Flexin' In Hell

Flexin' In Hell

Jeff Kelly

| ISBN: | Softcover | 978-1-4931-4776-2 |
| | eBook | 978-1-4931-4777-9 |

Disclaimer

The names and 'nick-names' mentioned in this little book have been totally made-up and are therefore *fictitious*. However, the reported actions connected to these **Fictitious** characters are completely true and have been Recounted exactly at these incidents happened. The opinions expressed in this book are the author's opinions only and are not officially endorsed by the Georgia Department of Juvenile Justice, or by the Georgia State Department of Education or by the publishing, Xlibris.

Print information available on the last page.

Rev. date: 11/25/2015

To order additional copies of this book, contact:
Xlibris
1-888-795-4274
www.Xlibris.com
Orders@Xlibris.com
551934

CONTENTS

Dedication

I dedicate this book to all of my former Teacher-Colleagues at the Paulding RYDC. I thank each of you for your humor and your constant support and assistance. During your teaching days at the RYDC, you have each probably worked many wonders and perhaps even a miracle or two! Only you know the special 'wins' that you have unofficially recorded. But you'll probably never be recognized for it. That's just the 'culture'. However, I want you to know that I do know it and so here's a special 'shout-out' for all of the special efforts you have each made just to show-up and to survive another day. Great job! Well done! And a Honkin' Big WHOOP!

And the same to all DJJ Teachers and JCOs everywhere!!! **Whooooooop!!**

Author's Note: The Lame-Ass cartoons within this book (pages: 32, 41, 61, 109 and the cover were created and drawn by the author.)

Acknowledgements

To Rokki C., my former classmate and old friend, for your enthusiastic encouragement and especially wise editorial input. You wouldn't let me quit when I was just too worn down and had become stalled due to all the depravity and frustration I was experiencing.

To "The Mountie Girl", Lady Haig for your ongoing support, enthusiasm and ego-stroking that inspired me to continue with this effort. You showed me what was possible as you keep on truckin' though life to your own very special Be-Bop rhythms!

To Jackie B. (who was another DJJ Teacher who became a new and such a joyful friend). You knew what it was like! And you always kept me laughing while we were sitting through all of those deadly seminars!

With special heartfelt gratitude to eight of my fraternity bros. Who each chipped in with a little financial support to help make this little book happen. I am eternally grateful.

- Bob-O "The Flying Marine"
- "Penguin"
- "Hoser"
- "Dr. Fisch"
- "Boosh" Rhythm King I
- "Kirk" Rhythm King II
- "Licky D"
- "Parksy" The Marathon Man

I love you guys!

Ístorikos

Pergé!

And finally to all four of my wonderfully supportive, loving and beautiful children, you have always been my biggest fans! You inspire me, you complete me and each and every single one of you fill my heart with swing!

Glossary of Terms

ADD Attention Deficit Disorder

ADHD Attention Deficit Hyperactivity Disorder

I.E.P Individual Education Plan

SEBD Severe Emotional Behavior Disorder

MID Mildly Intellectually Disabled

AEPM Alternative Education Management plan {The Detention Center equivalent of I.S.S, or In-school suspension)

Lock-Down Students who have misbehaved to such a severe extent over a brief period of time are locked into a series of special cells or back to their own cells for a day or two.

DJJ Department of Juvenile Justice (each state has one).

DR Disciplinary Report

SIR Special Incident Report is a special form which is used to document incidents such as, injuries, self-harm behaviors, suicide attempts, fights, property destruction, terroristic threats to staff, etc.

JCO Juvenile Corrections Officer. All JCOs are trained in First Aid, CPR and must be 'mandated' by completing special training in all forms of Physical control measures.

Introduction

When I first envisioned writing this book, I was concerned that the subject matter might become a little too grim for certain readers.But as things began to play out, I realized that I was beginning to accumulate enough bits of subject matter that could be strung together to make for an interesting and hopefully, a little bit funny, book. But put it together I did! Perhaps it was primarily a cathartic exercise to purge myself of all the miserable, frustrating and depressing moments that I was experiencing every day as a teacher in a pretty ugly place. I don't normally think of myself as funny at all, but I am always looking for the"funny" in everyday experiences. (good and bad.)

I soon began to realize that a little bit of humor placed here and there might be helpful in lightening-up the subject matter and further enhancing the reader's interest.

Most importantly, I also felt that I needed to provide for the reader a general understanding about how Public Education is carried out on a daily basis in Juvenile Detention Centers all throughout America. This book is not an exposé but it certainly does shine a light on a dark underside of American Public Education of which most most laypersons are unaware.

Furthermore, I also wanted to provide useful information for parents and educators about slang for street drugs and gang identifiers, etc. (See Appendix)

In August 2007, I commenced my teaching employment within a Regional Juvenile Detention Center as a Special Education Teacher with a prison staffing and management company.. **(Youth Services International, Inc.)** I was not a "Certified" Special Education teacher, but I am a Georgia "Certified" Social Studies Teacher(6-12).**NOTE**: In Georgia, all "Certified" teachers are required to have taken and passed a course in "Teaching The Exceptional Student." Subsequently, I received a "Provisional Certification" in Special Education, under which I was to teach Language Arts and five (5) different Science courses to various students at different grade levels. (Well I did spend nearly forty years in executive-level positions within the healthcare industry and I do have a lot of life experience!)

After retiring from all of the pressures resulting from trying to survive seven (7) seperate acquisitions and mergers along with the financial failures of so many cash-starved,healthcare organizations, I decided to go back to college for a second Degree! A degree that would enable me to become a "Certified Teacher" (NOTE: I had somehow survived and miraculously recovered from a serious medical event in1998. This scary time produced a blazing epiphany that I needed to change everything about my personal lifestyle. My original B.A. degree was from Colgate University in 1960 where I had majored in fine Arts. My new B.S. degree in Social Studies Education was achieved at Kennesaw State University in May 2005.

During the writing of this book I considered myself to be a very fit man at 6'1" and 225 lbs. and I exercised daily. Supposedly, I looked 10 or 15 years younger than my actual age. Or, "so they' say!" A full head of hair, daily exercise and some occasional applications of *Grecian Formula*™ has worked wonders. Unfortunately, I soon realized that despite all of the various County School Systems' disclaimers and denials about age discrimination, *Age Discrimination* was and still is, a constant! I couldn't even gain an interview for published "open" Social Studies teaching positions even though I had stated on my resume and various counties' applications, a willingness and capability to coach as many as five (5!) separate sports!! Furthermore, I am College Board "Endorsed" to teach Advanced Placement World History. Unfortunately, one just can't hide one's age because all of the School Systems' application forms require job history, college degrees,years of military service *including all **DATES***. Consequently, the occasional school administrator might glean the following from my application, *Goodness gracious! That boy must be in his late 60's!*

And the hiring administrators probably looked at my official application and probably concluded; too fixed in his ways, possibly unhealthy, technologically incompetent, and probably can't relate to the younger generation.

Excuuuse Me???

Consequently, personal finances and eight years of disastrous economic results from 'W's *'Voodoo Economics'* dictated that I must accept the first teaching job that came along. And so I did.

Foreword

On the cover of this book I have depicted a poker hand of playing cards which is known as "The Dead Man's Hand." (Two black aces and two black eights) According to Western legend, these are the cards that were held by the legendary Wild Bill Hickock when he was shot dead by some other low-life while playing poker. I have chosen "The Dead Man's Hand" to ironically symbolize the grim and deadly circumstances that the large majority of Juvenile DetentionCenter inmates everywhere were probably born into; Purely by a cosmic accident of birth. Most of the student/inmates depicted within this anecdotal book were probably born into this cruel world by parents who just did not have the educational, or financial abilities to rise above their own "accidents of birth." Perhaps the never-ending cycle of generation after generation of illiteracy, racism, criminality, drug addiction and feelings of inadequacy resulted in lives of grinding poverty and a debilitating cynicism.

Such a toxic environment creates an attitude, or an outlook that traps each child into a state of hopelessness, racial hatred and more than likely, a future life of crime. If the parents were smokers, alcoholics, or drug abusers, or if the mother did not receive adequate pre-natal care, then one can safely assume that the birth results would be disastrous. (Low to marginal intelligence, physical disabilities and possibly, behavior disorders). Under **I.D.E.A.** (The **Individuals with Disabilities Education Act)**. Public School Systems are mandated by the federal government to provide a free and equal education to students with recognized disabilities in the least restrictive environment.Such "exceptional students" are therefore eligible for "Special Education" status. NOTE: Only a relatively small portion of Detention Center students are designated for Special Ed. services. While most of these young individuals' unfortunate birth circumstances had placed them into neighborhoods where quality of life values were severely lacking. However, there was always an occasional student/inmate that might have 'been born into a more positive and supportive family environment; probably all they had done wrong was usually something totally stupid such as statutory rape, or drug possession. Some of us, the "fortunate ones", were brought up within loving families and in quality neighborhoods. We were provided with a support system that created a positive life outlook that stemmed from being surrounded by other high quality people. We were exposed to a value system that revered higher education and a strong work ethic. We learned to subscribe to strong moral values that totally rejected addictive habits, shortcuts and criminality.

Unfortunately, most of the youths being taught in Juvenile Detention Centers are faced with grim futures that boil down to three basic probabilities:

1. An early death (from murder, illness, or drug overdose).
2. A life spent totally behind bars in prison systems.
3. Or, miraculously, Educational progress that results in the beginnings of a productive career and hopefully, a better life!

Occasionally a spark of real potential is recognized and then carefully nurtured by good-hearted teachers and coaches everywhere. It is what teachers do. The sapling has been bruised and we must now do our very best to bring it back to a healthier strength that can allow it to grow and ultimately, thrive. Every now and then, we Detention Center Teachers, and other teachers and coaches everywhere, will actually win a precious few!

Chapter One

Welcome to Hell!

The slang term, *'Flexin"* means dat you be lyin'. Hell, everyone in dese places is 'flexin" all da time; <u>Including da teechurz!</u>

Author's NOTE: That first sentence is purposely written in prisonese. I just wanted you, dear reader, to start off with a little taste. But be careful, the rest of this little book is filled with all sorts of ugly thoughts and the worst possible language.

Now, if you are easily offended by nasty and foul language, you probably need to set this book aside and well away from young and innocent eyes. I don't normally use such foul language. I'm just a reporter here. So if you're still with me, come on in and jump into this cesspool, but be sure to hold your nose! Teaching in a Juvenile Detention Center has little resemblance to teaching in a public school and is certainly not at all like teaching in a private school! We catch the public school failures at the tail-end. We are the last resort. We get the dropouts and the rejects from Alternative schools. And finally, we get the newly incarcerated juvenile criminals (murderers, rapists, drug dealers,armed robbers, sodomists and pedophiles,you name it). Basically all of these so-called "students" started to fail way back in the early grades in public school. Many just moved forward through various grade levels via 'social promotion'. In general they are angry. Damn angry! That's for sure. They are frustrated and highly volatile. Common sense is in such short supply as to be nearly invisible. Sudden outbursts and tantrums are commonplace.

Many of these students have reading difficulties and far too many can't even read at all! General Math courses are reasonably easy except for those with mildly, or severely impaired intelligence As for me, I am a 'Certified' Social Studies Teacher, but I did not teach Social Studies! We already had two perfectly good Social Studies teachers in here. (One, General Ed. and one Special Ed. Both are great guys and fine teachers).

Consequently, Upon my hiring, I received a "Provisional Certification" to teach Special Education-designated students. In this capacity I taught various grade level Language Arts and Literature/Composition courses. Plus, I taught five (5) other Science courses; Physical Science, Biology, Life Science, Earth Science and General Science to various grade levels. Well, I do have two separate college degrees to go along with a forty plus (40+) year career as an "executive" in the healthcare industry. So I guess I have some unusual credentials that many younger and less experienced teachers just don't have. Mostly, I have what I believe to be especially strong "Leadership Skills". And **THAT** more than anything else, is what a Juvenile Detention Center Teacher must have. Of course, patience and a good sense of humor are sub-components within strong leadership skills. We Juvenile Detention Center teachers are "tested" mentally, emotionally and even physically every single class day! Consequently, if you can't lead effectively you will be run-off with your tail tightly tucked between your legs. (I've seen it happen.)

Teaching in a Juvenile detention Center is extremely frustrating. In fact, it is especially dangerous. Discouragement hits the new teacher early in his/her first several weeks. You just get so darned sick and tired and disgusted because of all the depravity that you see and hear. So many of the so-called students will throw down their assigned class-work onto the floor. Usually accompanied by an outburst something like this, *"Don't put that shit in front of me!"*

The old saying about leading a horse to water is consistently confirmed over and over again. This is simply not a much fun job.

Apparently, the worst thing you can be called here is *"Bitch"*. As in, *"You're a pussy-ass bitch."* Or, *"I'll get you, you pussy-ass bitch!"* I guess this all started from someone's immense anger and a momentary loss for words. You're a pussy and a bitch and just to express themselves more strongly they throw in 'ass'. Thus we have, . . ."*Pussy-ass bitch"*.

The heating and cooling system in the Paulding RYDC was so archaic that the classrooms were often much too hot in the summer months, or much too cold in the winter months.

Selanno's weather Report: "Man it's cold as fuck!"
I wonder, How cold is . . ."fuck?"

Chapter Two

When is the Racism Ever Going to End?

Racism abounds in this hell-hole. If you're a white teacher, to most of the black students you must be a "racist". As it turns out, it is primarily the black students that carry around an excess of toxic, racist baggage. As an educated, white teacher in authority, I was pretty much the "enemy" for each new black student that was entering my classroom for the first time. As a brand new student enters my classroom, I might receive a lovely initial greeting such as, *"Fuck you! . . . Bitch!"*. Racism seems to be such an easy excuse for failure in life.

To make matters even worse, I along with all of my other teacher colleagues, had also identified two black, female JCOs who obviously harbored major racial resentments against the predominantly white teaching staff. We college-degreed teachers are lower-paid relative to other "certified" teachers elsewhere, but we certainly earn more than the JCOs and they (The JCOs) know it. We teachers and JCOs are supposed to function as a 'team', but it is hard to be supportive teammates when the working relationships become racially frayed. I felt that I always got along great with most of the JCOs, but the two aforementioned female JCOs, obviously harbored a whole lot of hostility and anger towards the white teachers. That hostility was palpable. Unfortunately, these two were charged with the responsibility of dealing with Disciplinary Reports and then deciding what form of discipline would be administered to the offenders. If a white teacher wrote a DR on a student, (White or black) nothing ever happened to the offending student. Were these two JCOs 'on the take'? who knows? But I and many other teaching colleagues, not only felt that it was possible, but that it was quite probable! All it would take would be for a relative, or a friend of an inmate to give one of these two JCOs some money, or a little contraband off-site at a meeting place well away from the Detention Center. After all . . . How in the world does marijuana get in her? It's sure as hell not via the teaching staff!

Well, on second thought, ... maybe a long toke on some *"Mendicino Greeno"* might be just the thing to help a frazzled teacher mellow out at the end of the day! . . . (Hey!! **Just kidding!**)

We teachers would always get severely chastised if we so much as gave a student a left over snack from our lunch. I doubt that things are much different at other Juvenile Detention Centers.

One of the things that worked well for me was that during the run-up to the 2008 Presidential Election, I sent a check for $50.00 to the Democratic National Committee. Soon thereafter I received a glossy photo of President Obama and Vice-President Biden with the salutation underneath stating thanks for my *'extraordinary contribution!'* A color copy of the photo immediately went up upon the wall behind my desk and soon became a visually strong proof of me putting my money where my mouth was. Over the following months I would print extra color copies, minus the salutation, and give them to whichever students or JCOs wanted them. This pretty much silenced the "racist" taunts. Later in 2009, an additional $25.00 donation elicited another glossy photo of the swearing-in ceremony!

If you're a white inmate, you might get called *"Ku Klux"*. Not a good thing to be called. Sometimes a white inmate might call another white inmate *"Ku Klux.* These were pretty nasty attempts to put the other inmate in deep shit with the black inmates, or maybe the instigator is just trying to ingratiate himself with the black inmates. (Survival #101).

One incredibly stubborn and MID youth (see Glossary of Terms), Charlie, was stupid enough to put up a poster of the Confederate Battle flag upon the wall of his cell. Poor Charlie would tell others that he was not a racist Ku Kluxer and that it was only his South Carolina cousins who were members of the Klan. Maybe that Racist Wacko, Dylann Ruff who later on murdered all those black Church Members in Charleston, SC was one of Charlie's cousins! As if that totally exonerated him! How dumb was that? This only meant to the blacks that he came from an entire family of Ku Kluxers! Charlie was just too stubborn and too proud and just too MID to understand why his rebel flag poster had caused him to receive so much grief from the black inmates. Poor Charlie was constantly getting shoved, elbowed and slapped which made his time in here so much more difficult than it needed to be. I tried to tell him quietly that he needed to get that stupid Confederate Flag poster down, but he just wouldn't do it. I found Charlie to be a quite likeable young guy and his desk soon gravitated closer and closer until it abutted up against my desk. Charlie really liked to draw and he soon learned that I was also an artist. (not a great one, but reasonably accomplished). Perhaps Charlie felt safer sitting near to me, or probably he just wanted to share with me his many efforts at drawing trucks, trucks and more trucks. All of which sported Confederate Battle Flags! There were constant attempts to goad Charlie into a fight and many was the time that I would whisper, *"Do not respond! Donot respond!"* Apparently Charlie had engaged in sex with a younger girl and he ended up charged with statutory rape. The father of the girl brought all the charges. Poor stupid, stubborn Charlie thought he was going to get out soon and then get back together to hook-up with his little girlfriend. Lots of luck! With all due respect to the old "Chicken of the Sea" ™Tuna fish ad,. . . *"Sorry Charlie!"*

The Management Company (**Youth Services International**) that managed the Paulding RYDC was primarily staffed by African-Americans who held most of the important management positions; including the Detention Center Administrator and the Director of Security. On the other hand, the Education Dept. (Teachers, Assistant Administrator and Administrative staff) was virtually 100% white.

For a short while we had only one extremely pleasant and certainly effective, African-American teacher from Jamaica. This woman was recognized with the "Outstanding Teacher" Award . . . . Hmmmm?

Before this starts to sound too much like sour grapes on my part. I will certainly admit to the fact that I liked and respected this very pleasant teacher and it was clear that her students liked and respected her also. So I think she was probably deserving of the recognition. But for my money, "Mr. D" was clearly the best teacher in the place. The Detention Center Administrator, was on a big ego trip and clearly loved the sound of her own voice. Once she started into one of her addresses to the entire staff it was as if there was a never-ending tape-loop running inside her. Butts shifted, heads lolled and eyes rolled as she just continued to drone on and on. One particular presentation went on and on to the point of keeping the entire facility staff in the facility's gym for at least a full hour past the teachers' normal quitting time! It was always pretty obvious to the mostly white teaching staff that we just weren't that valued in her eyes. It finally dawned upon me, and I have to admit that it took awhile,

that she was running a PRISON and THAT always had to be her #1
priority. The mandated School within the detention center was probably
nothing more than a nuisance. One of our administrator's favored
accomplices was the book keeper, Ms. Ibukaba whom I had managed
to totally piss-off because she had clearly bollaxed my travel expense
reimbursement for two different weeks of mandatory DJJ training.
and I "called her out". Turns out she had either purposely postponed
or delayed, or had misplaced all of the teachers' expense reports. It was
only after my persistent pursuit of justice for the entire teaching staff and
my enlisting of the powerful support of the Senior Vice President, did
we teachers finally get reimbursed a full month later and well after the
fact! Apparently, the Senior V.P. had really dug in to resolve an obvious
book-keeping mess.

I'm quite sure Ibukaba felt that all because of me, she had probably
gotten herself pretty severely flayed. Ibukaba managed to survive, so
it seemed that our Administrator, had obviously protected her favored
accomplice while stupid, stubborn me had now created a deceptively
powerful enemy. After surviving nearly forty plus years of office politics
as an executive in the private sector, I should have known better!
However, the fact remained that several hundred dollars of legitimate
non-reimbursed travel expenses had placed me and several other
financially struggling teachers into a financial bind. Could this have been
just one more manifestation of racial animosity directed against the all
white teaching staff?

Okay I'll admit it; I can get stubbornly combative, particularly when
I recognize dishonest and unethical behavior. I seem to have consistently
demonstrated a life-long pattern throughout my working career of
doggedly pursuing justice in order to right obvious wrongs.

Chapter Three

Survival Skills

Many new student/inmates would walk right into my classroom, stare straight at me(The teacher) and loudly pronounce, *"Fuck you!"*

Well it's so nice to see you too!" Or he or she might announce to all others present that, *"I'm buckin' today!"* Which means he or she (Usually a she, like "'The Mouth") is going to be totally obnoxious; won't do a thing they are asked and will probably ultimately end-up in lockdown. You will meet *'The Mouth'* later on but "Buckin" seems to be an everyday thing with certain female students. Perhaps they are mad at somebody or some thing. (could it be P.M.S? . . . Possible). Maybe something happened over night, or it could just be a simple case of "mean girls". Or maybe it was bad news from home. Who knows? If it's not a lie to get out of trouble, the inmates are constantly *flexin'* as long and as loud as they can about how bad-ass tough they are. Of course the volume of flexin' braggadocio and posturing goes up ten-fold if just one new student is added to the class. All of these characters are in constant fear of being attacked or bullied and therefore, they can't seem to stop running their nasty and vulgar mouths. Threats abound, but frankly it's all a bunch of crap. Basically, they are all cowards and will bully anybody they think they can intimidate. You rarely see an inmate mouthing off to or threatening a bigger inmate. Fights are over quickly. Usually it's a sucker punch from behind, or when a JCO is nearby to break up the fight before the instigator can get his sorry ass totally and deservedly kicked. Actually not many guys in here really know how to use their fists. They think they do, but mostly they don't. what you usually see is a lot of wind-milling, but very few straight and hard punches with real leverage.

Most often such punches are sucker punches referred to in here as a "sneak." If somebody got "sneaked" it means he got slugged when he wasn't looking.

Gang activity is a constant and is mostly divided along racial lines. A black "gang-banger" wannabe might be required to put a "sneak" on a targeted white guy (This happened twice in my classroom). One particularly hateful and obnoxious black, the "'Tub of Goo", just got up from his desk and splat! Slugged square in the nose a totally unsuspecting white student, who was quietly doing his assignment: It was the most sickening sound and the victim's nose was broken. Of course the victim's eyes automatically watered and so the black gang instigators(Crips) gave the victim a lot of crap about crying. Later on when the "Tub of Goo" learned that the mother of the assaulted victim was going to press charges, he himself broke down in tears! What a sniveling and disgusting coward was the "Tub of Goo!" You will read more about the 'Tub of Goo' further on regarding the time when he tried and failed to bust my face with a thrown encyclopedia book!

Many of the girls in here are either infected with STDs, or are pregnant. Virgins are probably non-existent. Sadly, female self-esteem is at rock-bottom. It seemed to me that so many of the black girls just seem mad as hell and consequently, acted out a lot and when the female inmates did, oh my! All the girls, white and black, were so LOUD! You could hear the high-pitched cursing and screaming all over the place even with the classroom door closed! Of course, such high pitched screaming immediately triggered a mad rush to the classroom door by all of the male student/inmates in a futile attempt to find out who was being attacked, or being forcibly removed by the JCOs to lockdown. So many of the female inmates are so desperately needy in terms of love and of course, they are bored. Therefore, much of their school time was spent in passing and receiving notes back and forth with the male inmates.

Probably half, or almost all, of the female inmates had been sexually abused by their dad, or mom's boyfriend, or their stepfathers, or their uncles, cousins, or brothers. These female inmates seem to feel that all they have going for them is their sexuality and that "ultimate weapon" they can so easily use to control the males of the species. This way of thinking makes them so vulnerable. I often wondered how many had been picked-up off the mean streets on charges of prostitution.

Occasionally one might recognize a rare female JCO that could be semi-attractive, but all that such female JCOs got for their troubles were just a lot of nasty and rude comments about their booty.

I had one younger male student in my first period class who would always be one of the first to enter my classroom. Whereupon, he would immediately commence to shift around five or six desks until he had created a large barrier around his desk that was placed in the back corner of my classroom. It was very similar to a small fort. As I thought longer about this strange behavior, I finally realized that this was just a defense mechanism to delay a sudden assault from whomever might come into the room with bad intentions. This moving around of all my desks at the start of the school day was a small Problem. I needed adequate spacing between students. (Believe me, you always needed to maintain enough space between certain students and especially whenever there were "mixed" Co-Ed classes with boys and girls present (see Epilogue).

Another thing that most of the students would do was to sharpen their pencils to the sharpest point possible. They would usually try to retain these pencils rather than turn them in at the end of the class period. They would toss the pencils upward to see if they would stick point first into the suspended ceiling tiles. (Sharp enough to plunge into somebody's neck, or to use as protection if "sneaked.") Of course I was always buying pencils and pencil sharpeners.

Every now and then the Bi-Polar, Weezer (One of the worst of the worst)would try to steal and run-off with one of my sharpeners, which were fastened to a long table with a vacuum seal. Weezer would immediately smash the sharpener into pieces and try to extract the razor-like blade within.

As it turns out I can now recall four separate planned and sudden assaults that occurred within my classroom! In two such cases I was able to physically intervene, but most of the time I was too late and stuck in my chair behind my desk.These were not just classroom flare-ups, or your normal day-to-day fights that started over a perceived insult or some other aggravation. No, these were planned and coordinated assaults! I always felt a deep responsibility to protect everyone in my classroom and I repeatedly stated that if they were attacked, that I would be the first one to jump into the fray to try to protect the victim. I felt I was still physically fit enough to make good on my promise. I hoped that once they all believed my commitment to them, maybe they would be the first ones to protect me if I was under assault. Naïve? Perhaps so.

Later on however, I came to my senses with the bothersome realization that there would always be one or two of the "Worst of the worst" who would not lift a single finger to help me. These few bad-ass types were totally devoid of any sense of loyalty, or a sense of how and when to do the "right thing;" no matter how well someone might have treated them. They were just bad dudes and rotten to the core. They were what they were (sociopaths).

As a teacher, in a Detention Center, you're either "cool," or you're an asshole. I guess I might have passed the "cool" test, but to a few hard cases, I am sure I must have come off as an asshole. Most of the time the male students would usually sit with their hands pushed down under the waistband of their loose and non-belted jeans. Belts and shoelaces are non-existent.(No suicides allowed!) Handshakes in here? Not happening! At least not from me! *"No! I won't shake your hand! Not while it's been hanging on to all your junk down there!"*

So fist bumps in a funky, step-by-step order become the standard method for respectful greetings in a detention center.

Bump, bump, bump and then a final knuckles-to-knuckles twisting motion to symbolically "lock it in".

Sometimes a particularly angry student would storm into my classroom feigning great anger at me. They would usually state something like *"You wrote a DR on me!"* (Disciplinary Report) My response? *"No, you wrote a DR for yourself by your totally intolerable behavior!"* Funny how twisted are their thought processes. The inmate/students have such a hard time controlling their emotions and understanding that it is their own stupid behavior that constantly gets them in trouble. Certain behaviors absolutely cannot ever be tolerated by any teacher. Nevertheless, in these twisted minds, the awarding of a DR must be the teacher's or the JCOs fault! Or, as my Special Ed. teacher colleague "Lieut. Dan" sees such behavior as just a reflection of a chronic Detention Center syndrome. He has termed it "JPS Syndrome." (Just Plain Stupid).

Chapter Four

The Soldiers Who Shared My Foxhole

I guess I should commence this chapter with an explanation of how our particular Detention facility was so ineptly managed. There were three Special Ed teachers, myself included, who were staffing three Special Ed.Classrooms that were connected in a row along what was known as the Special Ed. Hall. My classroom was placed squarely in the middle and this location caused me considerable extra problems. (see diagram pg. 33) The "problems" I refer to primarily emanated from two different causes. Number one neither teacher on either side of me was physically capable of preventing their Special Ed. students from walking out of their classrooms and into my classroom. If they had situated themselves in their classroom doorways, the students would probably just get into the teacher's desks and steal whatever they could get their thieving hands on. (As I proceed to describe my two Special Ed, teaching colleagues you will understand why they were both so physically limited). The second part of each of our security "problems" stemmed from the fact that our employer (YSI) in a misguided attempt to operate "on the cheap," refused to staff the Special Ed. classrooms with any guard (JCO) presence. The best we could hope for was that there might be an occasional JCO assigned to cover the Special Ed.hallway. Most of the time, in fact, there was very little if any JCO presence in the Special Ed. Hall area! What was so frustrating for me was that any kind of intelligent analysis by management would have clearly shown that the Special Ed. area was the internal school area that had an inordinate number of "special incidents" that were extremely serious and too often involved major assaults, or "'sexual" incidents. Special Ed. was where students defined as having Severe Emotional Behavior Disorder were present.

Any fool could have understood that two of the three Special Ed. teachers were not only physically unable to protect themselves, but they were also physically unable to protect other students in their classrooms from student-on-student assaults. A JCO presence in the Special Ed. classrooms would have greatly reduced the ongoing and far too numerous "incidents" that were always happening in the special Ed. classrooms. Consequently, I became pretty unpopular with upper management because I was turning into a discomfitting "whistleblower" who continued to create written documentation about the inadequate security coverage in the Special Ed. area. I guess, in hindsight, that my insistence in consistently documenting that the *'Emperor had no clothes'* probably doomed me to a bad end.(I just wanted my children to have enough legal documentation in case I was either killed, or incapacitated.

"Lieut. Dan": was stricken with childhood polio and has been wheelchair-bound ever since. He became a great and true friend and was, in many ways, my Special Education mentor. 'Lieut. Dan' was the Special Ed. Social Studies Teacher. His wry and sardonic sense of humor can often border on sarcastic, but was always clever and well placed. 'Lieut. Dan' has an especially deep interest, or fascination in all things of a military nature. Weapons, history of weaponry, war histories and war films seem to be among his greatest interests. Hence, I bestowed upon him the military rank of Lieutenant.Whenever we had ended a conversation and were returning to our classrooms, or leaving for the day, one of his favorite sayings, *"Keep 'em flying!"* was right out of the patriotic posters from the WWII era. He also might bark out *"Battle Stations!"* whenever our lunch-hour break had ended and we could hear students entering the education halls for their afternoon classes.

'Lieut. Dan' had previously been a disc jockey in Tampa, Florida. and had a wealth of knowledge about popular music. Dan often amazed me with his uncanny ability to recall the lyrics of old 60's and 70's Rock songs. Since I am also a certified Social Studies teacher and the proud owner of a huge and eclectic music collection, we had a wealth of common ground that we often shared. Lieut. Dan has two very thick and powerful arms from all those years of propelling himself and his manual wheelchair around. If he ever got one of those bozos'head in a headlock,he could crack it just like using a nutcracker!

Finally, Lieut. Dan was fortunate to obtain a used power chair for sale at a deep discount. Frankly, I don't know how I could have gotten through those god-awful days without Lieut. Dan's humor, support and encouragement. We helped each other.

Here is **Lieut Dan':** Rolling by in his wheelchair and leaving for home. *"Man, I've had a month of a day!"* or, this one when the school-day had ended and the student/inmates were lined up in the main hallway for the routine pat-down. 'Lieut. Dan' whizzed past and down the hall in his brand new power chair. One of the inmates went, *"Vroom Vroom!"* I couldn't help but smile and tried to cover it up but this only got several of the characters laughing about my seeing the humor in the 'vroom, vroom'. Well, it was funny to me at the time.

"The Big O": I'm not talking about female orgasms or professional Basketball superstars here. 'The Big O' is just a fitting euphemism for my other Special Ed. friend and colleague who taught Math/Algebra/Geometry in the classroom next door to mine. Unfortunately, 'The Big O' was grossly obese.(Possibly approaching 300+ lbs or more!) Thus, my poor and insensitive attempt at a little humor here while I try not to give away her true last name which started with an O. I always felt terribly sorry for her because these guys would go out of their way to be cruel and hurtful. They would constantly engage in asking the crudest personal questions such as *"How do you and your husband have sex?"* And they all loved to imitate the way she walked and how she always had to call out *"Officerrrr"* from her classroom doorway.

One day as the "Big O" was struggling down the main hallway to go home, while the inmates were leaning up against the wall for pat-down, I heard one of the inmates bark out, *"Fat ass!"* (Nice!) So many of these characters could be so heartless and immature and totally lacking in empathy, or conscience.How that poor woman could go home each day without dissolving into tears, I will never know. When I asked her, she told me with a tone of determination and firm resolve, *"I will never, ever let them see me cry!"* This is a good woman who is kind and who does as well as she can given the lack of support that she doesn't get from Management. I would often tell her to not take it personal because it was probably just a reflection of the students' hatred for Algebra.

Oh well, so it goes. She somehow let herself get this way and this is obviously a rough place to work and she had worked here once before. She knew the deal. I like 'The Big O' and as time went by, she became a good and supportive friend. I often worried that her heart could give out at any moment. The blood pressure that must already be far too high and the strain on her heart must go through the roof whenever the adrenalin kicks in. Believe me,the adrenalin kicks in on an almost hourly basis for every teacher in here! I worry a lot for "The Big O."

"Mr. D." or "The Big Goombah": 'Mr. D.' is the General Ed. Social Studies Teacher (*Not* Special Ed). and he definitely gets my vote for **"Best Teacher in the Place."** I'm very fond of "Mr. D." (as the students call him). "'The Big Goombah" is just my term of endearment; even though he's not particularly large. Every lunch hour the three of us: me, 'Lieut. Dan' and 'Mr. D.' might meet and eat our lunches in 'Lieut. Dan's' classroom and 'Lieut. Dan' would flip that day's page in his desk calendar. On each page there would be some sort of historical trivia question for the day and we three Social Studies teachers would each take our best shot at answering it. If I had a streak of one or two in a row correct, I would make a big deal out of reminding one and all that I was now leading the league! 'Lieut. Dan' was usually pretty good at coming up with the answers to what seemed to be the most esoteric and trivial history questions.

On the other hand, I tended to get most of the sports-related questions while 'Mr. D.' pretty much killed on any and all questions that might have remotely involved Italian history or culture. Whenever 'Mr. D' was on a hot streak and had answered one more correctly, he would go into his "Cock of the Walk" impression.

This "act" consisted of shaking one widespread hand above his head like a rooster's comb and shaking the other widespread hand and thumb against his rear-end (supposedly like a rooster's tail-feathers.)To add further to his impression, he would strut like a rooster in a simulated scratching motion. This "'Cock of the Walk' routine, would usually end up with Lieut. Dan hysterically and repeatedly pounding his fist down upon his desk. Which action usually resulted in scattering all over the floor remaining greasy chicken bones from his fried chicken lunch.

I don't know what amused me more. Was it'Mr.D's' silly-ass routine, or was it how totally cracked up'Lieut. Dan' always became after taking in 'Mr. D's' barn-yard strut? (See my stupid cartoon of the 'Cock of the Walk')

I guess what impressed me most about 'Mr. D.' Was that he obviously knew his subjects very well and knew how to impart his knowledge in a very pleasant way. His patience with his students was incredible and he was such a very kind man. I could never have been so patient with some of the things I saw some students do while he was teaching.(keep in mind that most of his classes contained around twenty plus students at a time). Here's an example: "Mr. D" was preparing an eighth grade class in Georgia History for the upcoming CRCT standardized tests. I had been asked to sit-in and assist with the eighth grade students for that week's frantic Test preparations. While 'Mr. D.' was standing up and teaching in front of his class, one totally rude and obnoxious student just continued to walk around and around in front of 'Mr. D.' while continually shooting wadded up paper balls at 'Mr. D's' wastebasket. Mr. D.'never even blinked, or acknowledged what this particular jerk was doing! I clearly have never had that kind of patience and I just couldn't take it any longer; so I got up and escorted said 'Jerk' to AEPM.

It also seemed to me that the female students more readily sensed 'Mr. D's'patience and inherent kindness, so he was obviously a big favorite with them. 'Mr. D.' was particularly helpful to me early on when I had first arrived at the facility.I always appreciated mr.D's thoughtfulness, support and many kindnesses (Besides we both appreciated great old-time,smooth jazz such as Miles Davis and etc).

The "Cock of the Walk!"

So now that you know all about "'Lieut. Dan's" and 'The "Big O's," physical limitations, you should be able to understand why I had such a big problem with my classroom being situated right between their two classrooms; particularly when there was so little security coverage in the Special Ed. classrooms and the related hallway area.

General Education Classrooms

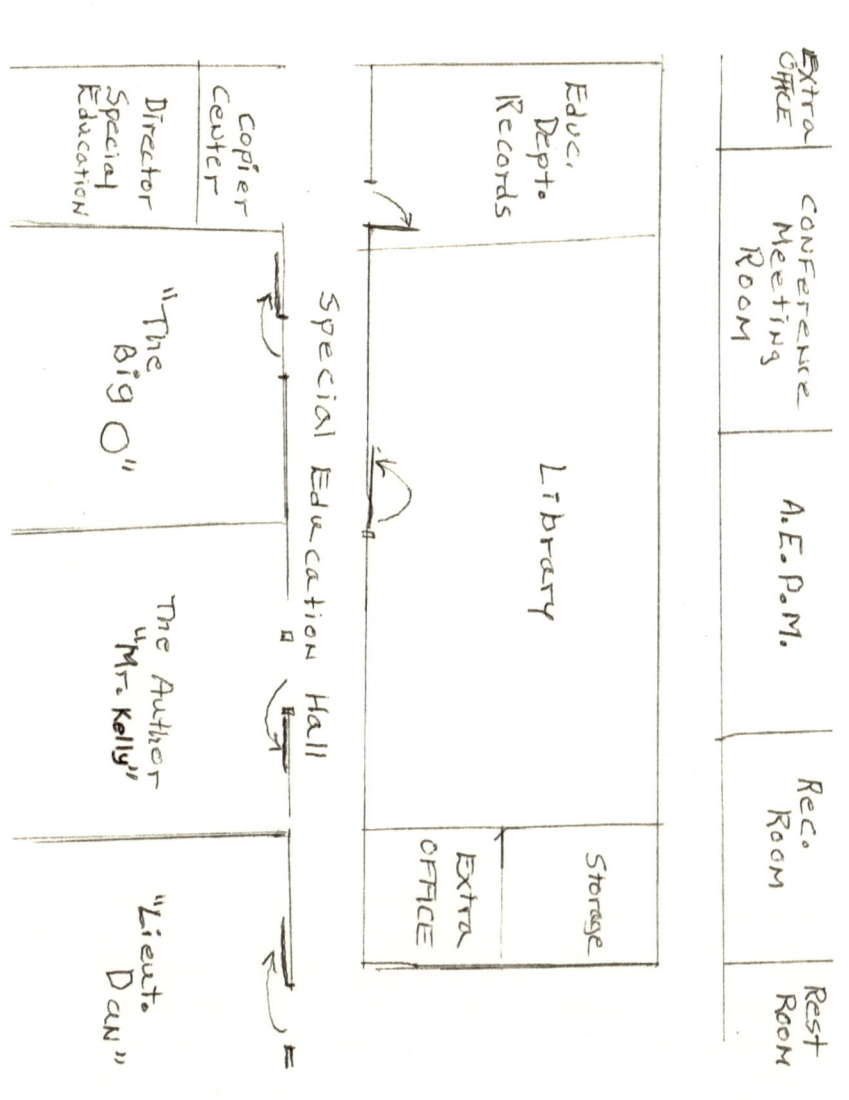

Extra Office

Conference Meeting Room

A.E.P.M.

Rec. Room

Rest Room

Educ. Dept. Records

Library

Storage

Extra Office

Copier Center

Special Education Hall

Director Special Education

"The Big O"

The Author "Mr. Kelly"

"Lieut. Dan"

Chapter Five

What da hell is a %*@*+** CAP?!

The newly entered students into each Georgia Juvenile Detention Center's Education System certainly must wonder about the answer to that question. However,the 'Frequent Fliers'are pretty much on top of understanding their CAP Progress. CAP is a Dept.of Juvenile Justice acronym that stands for **Curriculum Activity Packet.**

Here in Georgia, the State Dept.of Education's Professional Standards Commission establishes the chronological process about how each course's subject matter at each grade level will be taught. That does not necessarily refer to a teacher's personal teaching style. What it really means is that the teacher is responsible for following a road map in implementing the basic Professional Standards lessons for each subject and grade level that a Georgia student is expected to learn. The CAP system of class assignments is usually in the optimal sequence or logical progression that ultimately runs to the final completion of the course. Each CAP is directly tied to each Georgia Professional Standard for a given course of study in all of Georgia's school systems. CAPs are expressed in numerical sequence such as CAP1, CAP. 2, CAP 3, etc. An example of how this works might be in ninth grade Physical Science: CAP 1 might cover Gravity or CAP 2 might cover Friction, CAP 3 Energy, and so on.

For example, a student/inmate who is scheduled to take Physical Science (9) might have worked his/her way all the way up to CAP 27 with only three or four more CAPs to go before reaching "End of Course" testing.

In my Special Ed. classroom I might have been assigned up to eight or ten students per class period and they might each be of different ages. Thus, during any particular period, I could have a totally unrelated mix of students with each student involved in different courses from each other.Perhaps this is how old-time teachers in rural school houses taught way back in the olden times.

Here's an example of a potential student/inmate 'mix' in one of any given class period for special education students:

- A senior working on CAP 10 Environmental Science.
- A Junior working on CAP 3 Language Arts.
- A sixth grader working on CAP 15 Life Science.
- An eighth grader working on CAP 4 Earth Science.
- And finally, another junior working on CAP 5 Language Arts.

Consequently, there are relatively few moments when a Detention Center <u>Special Ed.</u> teacher is standing before a class and teaching the exact same subject matter to each student at the same time. The example I gave you above is typical of a special Ed.classroom involving fewer students. However, the example above does not hold totally true with regards to the General Education classes. In the various General Education classes at our facility, the teachers are usually teaching one primary subject such as Math, Language Arts, or Social Studies, etc. the Gen. Ed. class schedules are set-up to accommodate similar age groups. Consequently, a Social Studies teacher like 'Mr. D.' might be teaching 8th grade 'History of Georgia' to a group of eighth graders. A Gen. Ed. Math classroom of 20 students could also have several types of math being taught such as ninth and tenth grade Algebra.

Perhaps you can now more easily understand why I previously stated that the most important trait or skill that a Juvenile Detention Center teacher absolutely must have is clearly,

'STRONG LEADERSHIP SKILLS'. Each student has his/her own folder into which the required CAP sheets have been placed by the teacher. Once class starts, the students get their folders and text books and perform the required steps as designated by the CAP sheet. The numbered CAP sheet would name the textbook, the chapter, the pages to be read and then which End of Chapter questions the student must answer. My role as a Special Ed. teacher was basically one of 'expediter', or 'helper'. I often answered whatever questions a student might have about where to find the answers to the questions within the text they had just read. I would often have to answer questions such as, *"What does this word mean?"* or I might need to more fully explain a confusing concept, by use of an example.

(Slide a book across the floor to demonstrate friction or use the example of a cue ball imparting energy to an object ball, thereby demonstrating Kinetic energy). I might also try to explain how the present CAP relates to the previously completed CAP. When a student had completed his CAP work for that period it would be turned in for grading.

Theoretically, students in public schools are learning these very same lessons at the same time.Consequently, Juvenile Detention Center students have the opportunity to keep pace with their public school peers as long as they make legitimate attempts to maintain their CAP progress.

As I stated earlier, it is so extremely difficult to prod these types of non-motivated and profoundly discouraged students to commence working towards the satisfactory completion of a course. I had become immensely frustrated with my difficulties in 'selling' these hard cases on progressing in their schoolwork. So I remembered an old motivational ploy I had used in an earlier private sector position. I had done this with some nurses I had previously supervised who had been converted into quasi-salespersons. I made a conscious effort to publicize the nurses' weekly and monthly sales results. Consequently, I bought a rectangular whiteboard for my classroom and used some auto pin striping tape to separate students' names and classes by class period. On the whiteboard there would also be each student's current progress and grade points average for the course. This process really started to get plenty of attention and even generated a lot of bragging rights.

"Man, I be carryin' a grade of 90 and I'm up to CAP 24already! And you just draggin' yo ass!"

As they watched me post the daily scores and progress of each student, the attention level would rise considerably. There weren't many that liked being way down near the bottom. Amazingly, that whiteboard chart became almost magical!" the Detention Center teacher's role is basically to be informed and knowledgeable about each subject being taught, but it is also to maintain classroom order. Plus, you've got to ensure student/inmate safety at all times. And, oh yes! I almost forgot. The Detention Center teacher must certainly be a motivator. Selling skills are also important because by the end of each day you have probably spent quite a few minutes" "selling" to a bunch of non-receptive student/ inmates on why their education is so important. Yup! Teaching in a detention center is extremely challenging, frustrating and even dangerous. But,bottom-line, it will always require a whole bunch of strong leadership skills. That's for sure! It is certainly not for the faint-hearted.

Chapter Six

A Rogues Gallery

(these are the ones that were tough to love)

Claudius Blubberson: What an obnoxious S.O.B.! A hyperactive ADHD and overweight black who couldn't stay seated, always wandered out of the classroom and into the hall and tried to disappear. Claudius is overweight. (nice boobs). He is the worst kind of a bully and like most Bullies,he is most definitely a coward.

Again I will re-state the fact that our employer (Y.S.I.) Which staffed and managed the Detention Center under a contract with the Georgia Dept. of Juvenile Justice,was constantly trying to keep personnel costs as low as possible.

Consequently, there was virtually zero JCO coverage in the Special Ed. classroom area! The best we could hope for was one of the better JCOs to have Special Ed. hall duty which merely consisted of wandering around in the halls and being responsive if called. Conversely,JCOs were all around the General Education area either in the classrooms., or sitting on their rear ends in the Gen. Ed. hall. And that is why the Special Ed. classes were rife with problems because the ADHD kids were constantly wandering in and out of the classrooms with impunity and why Claudius wandered off whenever and wherever his fat-assed self wanted to go!

The scene:

I'm standing in the classroom doorway trying to keep my "hyper-actives" from leaving the classroom.

> 'Claudius Blubberson': *"Get out of my way bitch!"*
> Me: *"Get back to your desk, Claudius and sit down."*
> 'Claudius Blubberson': *"I'll go right through you!"*
> Me: *"Claudius you're not big enough, you're not tough enough and you're sure not quick enough, so back off! If you try it, you'll make somebody a very nice wife in big boy's prison!"*—
> 'Claudius Blubberson': *"Fuck you! You pussy-ass bitch!"*

Like I said before, if you let these birds think you're intimidated they will run you off for sure.

Another Claudius Blubberson story: I have since learned that after Claudius was released and out on the street that he had repeatedly threatened to shoot, or kill one of my white students (Wilbrooks) who comes from the same area. (more on Wilbrooks later)

One morning after 'Claudius Blubberson' was back in this joint all over again, a fight broke out in the cafeteria. 'Claudius ran over, aimed a quick kick at a white guy on the bottom of the melee and then quickly waddled away for cover. (Typical) I had previously warned Claudius that bullies always and inevitably get their comeuppance. Someday somebody smaller would almost certainly deck him. And someone finally did! HooHah! And Hallelujah!

As 'Lieut. Dan' so deftly put it, *"Some short little pile of white muscle popped him good!"*

Right behind 'Claudius Blubberson' in grossness and hatefulness was another fat-assed black who shall be known herein as "The Tub of Goo". This one was younger than many others in here. He is certainly obese, but not overly obese or as large as 'Claudius Blubberson'. "The Tub" has the filthiest mouth of all and will sit at his desk while sucking on the bottom of his tee shirt (Just like Linus of 'Peanuts' fame with his blanky). In doing so he exposes several rolls of fat around and upon his stomach. (Definitely not a pretty sight.) One day he entered the classroom with the worst case of B.O. imaginable. I noticed it immediately and the two female students present really made a huge fuss about it. (feigning gagging etc). Later on a female JCO entered the classroom with the astonished inquiry, *"Good God! Who brought in the funk?"* it was that bad! It was a beast! It had a life of its own! (sort of like the odiferous car that had been valet-parked in a classic Seinfeld' episode). Finally "The Tub if Goo" was removed to get cleaned up and to put on some fresh, new clothes. Thank God!

During one particular class period The Tub of Goo had been carrying on in the most filthy and disrespectful way.Another student, Dinsman, was trying to put together the exterior case of my computer, which had been broken previously. This happened when Weezer, another particularly hateful and **Bi-Polar** student, had thrown his desk at my desk. As the "Tub of Goo" was being escorted out of the room to AEPM by a JCO, the "Tub" grabbed a thick and relatively heavy encyclopedia book from the top of a file cabinet and threw it as hard as he could right at my face.He was only about ten feet away.

From an athletics Standpoint, I had always been blessed with pretty quick hands and those quick hands miraculously reacted just in time to catch the book on its edge just inches from my face! Had it hit my face it might have broken some facial bones or knocked me out, or at least caused the loss of a few teeth. "The Tub" was so frustrated by my miraculous catch that he grabbed another book and slung it in the same way. I knew it was coming this time, so I just ever so casually leaned my head to the left and watched the book fly past. The slow motion casualness of my head tilt away from the flying book, totally impressed Dinsman.

"Mr. Kelly that was soooo cool! . . . You just matrixed him!"

Dinsman's reference to being "Matrixed" was a pretty funny take on my slow motion move to avoid the flying book. Dinsman was referring to the hit movie *"The Matrix"* in which the star, Keanu Reeves, floats around in slow motion within a web-like matrix.

Darius: A Pretty tough guy. A real hard case. Highly dangerous and always threatening, or feigning suicide. Darius has a little drawing talent. In fact he is quite good. He specializes in elaborate and flowing printing styles.I'm sure that Darius is one helluva graffiti artist back in "the hood". One time I showed him some pencil drawings of mine that I had done while a Fine Arts major in college. My drawings were high detail renderings of my hand and also of my bare foot. So, lo and behold, during one class period, Darius showed up with a very nice pencil rendering in high detail of his hand! Despite my efforts to be civil, friendly and even inspiring to Darius, my reward was the following exchange:

> Darius: An arm's length away with a deadly serious and intimidating look while standing directly in front of my desk: *"I will kill you tomorrow."*
>
> Me: *"Well, Darius I guess I'd better bring my AK 47."*
>
> Darius: *"I've got an M16!"*
>
> P.B. *"Darius, knowing you, you'd probably shoot yourself in the foot just trying to load that thing!"*

Auzzen: Not much nice to say about this one except to say that he's not stupid. Auzzen is shifty-eyed and sort of a wiry redneck. He doesn't walk, he skulks! He always seems to be looking over his shoulder. He is so foul-mouthed and reprehensible that I look for a trail of slime as he moves along. Auzzen thinks he's tough but he's wiry/skinny and has no discernible fighting skills. Auzzen is certainly capable of sticking a shank into some poor unsuspecting soul. He continually swears as a JCO removes him out of my classroom to *AEPM,*. *"Someday I'm going to hit that old man!"*

Yeah Auzzen, go ahead . . . try it . . . I'd enjoy having you try that!

Twinkles: My nickname for this one. They don't come any more obnoxious than the passive-aggressive "Twinkles." Twinkles exudes an effeminate persona in the way he walks, talks and gestures . . . He is super hyperactive (ADHD) and manipulative to an extreme. Twinkles is a grand master at 'obnoxious'. Twinkles yells out anything he wants to say and is constantly being dragged off to AEPM. In each class he will try to drive the teacher crazy by making repeated demands, or demands for such items as, *"I want a pencil!"* Then, *"No, it's too short!"* Or, *"No, I want a black one!"* Or, *"No! It needs an eraser!"* then, *"I want a pink eraser, not a black one!"* Etc. Etc. Ad nauseum. And of course the foulest obscenities flow constantly. Twinkles is very much the jailhouse lawyer. He claims he knows every D.J.J. policy and injects his mistaken opinions into any corrective action a teacher needs to take with any misbehaving student, whether its Twinkles or not. This invariably causes Twinkles to blurt out,

"You can't do that! I'm going to write a grievance!" My normal response? *"Here's the form. You can't even spell grievance much less write one!"* Twinkles is the half and half product of a mixed birth. Consequently. he makes a big deal of being black.(Survival #101) He postures a lot and tries to project an image of being tough. One time, in Lieut. Dan's classroom, he 'sneaked'poor stupid Charlie and Charlie hit the floor. Twinkles is sort of upper body strong, but he is nowhere near to being athletic or coordinated. He hates P.E. and manipulates in any way he can to avoid it. Twinkles' limp-rested femininity comes out strongly as he loves to gossip and flex to make up anything he wants. He will take a small grain of truth and spin it into gospel fact. Apparently, twinkles father disappeared and his mother died during childbirth.

One of Twinkles older sisters is now his designated guardian and she has disowned him because she caught him sexually molesting her little two year old toddler boy! Twinkles is so obnoxious and hateful that I can't even stand the sight of him. (That's pretty bad for a teacher to admit and I feel guilty for saying it.) I guess that just goes with the territory. Teachers should be compassionate, patient and understanding. But the fact remains Twinkles has taken obnoxious to a higher art form. Twinkles struggles with a lot of self-self-image issues. Maybe he, or she is a Transgender male.

Weezer: This nasty, little, white and bi-polar bugger clearly exhibits SEBD and ADHD! (Nice combination!) He rarely takes his meds. He even tries to barter with other students quantities of Aderal, or Seroquel pills that he has hoarded and hidden. Weezer is another one of those students who you just hate to see enter your classroom such as 'Twinkles,' or The Beast.' Weezer will wander into any classroom whenever there is a female student present. He has a pretty good pop-out bicep when he decides to flex it.Consequently, he will willingly bully smaller white inmates. Weezer is clearly smarter than most of the other students and he maintains that he is at genius IQ! Huh?? What a bunch of hooey! He just seems like a genius when compared to the other JPS Syndrome residents. Weezer hates to read and therefore rarely does anything assigned in his Lit/Comp. reading assignments. He will readily fly through his Earth Science assignments and becomes quite hostile if I don't keep him busy and grade his work fast enough. He seems to have a fairly strong kinetic/mechanical intelligence. Weezer has even developed a crude tattooing device and seems to have created a small side business in that area. I wonder how many inmates contracted hepatitis, or some other nasty staph infection as a result of a Weezer tattoo. One morning Weezer continued to fuss about needing to go to the rest room. Unfortunately, there was no JCO around to escort him (as usual). So Weezer casually walked over to a corner of my classroom while smirking his obnoxious little smirk, pulled out his equipment and urinated all over the walls and floor in the corner! Another time he became so angry at me that he picked up a desk and threw it at my desk area. Thereby, knocking my computer, monitor, keyboard and mouse to the floor. The computer case was broken, but the hard drive remained unscathed.

Weezer is immensely proud of all of the hateful things he has done to various teachers, but mostly the other inmates think he's a little crazy. Weezer landed in here for statutory rape and he is totally pre-occupied with sex. Weezer is constantly talking about every vile thing imaginable that he might do to a girl. Any girl! He tries hard to flirt with the female JCOs and seems to think his obnoxious smirks and smiles are sexually appealing. I'll give him this, he does exhibit a little bit of a Ferris Buehler look. Weezer is only in sixth grade and is quite short.He is maybe five feet tall and that might be a stretch.

One day, Weezer went on and on flexing about how he had had sex in his cell one night with a female JCO. (Claimed *"Her butt was much too hairy!"*) *from this point on I will refer to her as Officer "Bristlebutt.".* Weezer will also go on and on endlessly about how he will become a millionaire entrepreneur. I listen patiently and try not to destroy his pipe dreams. The plan is that his company will pick up grease and cooking oils from restaurants and convert it into green energy not unlike diesel fuel. Supposedly Weezer's father physically abused and beat Weezer pretty severely. Dad is in prison. Weezer's birth mother, or his stepmother, is a "Hooters" waitress. There doesn't seem to be much love for either of them and there seems to be an ongoing custody battle between his physically abusive father and his birth mother, or stepmother. Looks like Weezer is gonna be Grandma's problem. If Weezer ever does get his life turned around, I seriously expect to read about him someday as a serial rapist, sexual harasser and etc. I would put nothing past him. He just has too many snakes writhing around in that twisted little head of his. Another big part of Weezer's obnoxiousness is his flagrant ass-kissing of the larger Alpha blacks. Weezer is the quintessential toady-sycophant. Obviously, I don't care much for this little guy. But what I mostly dislike about him is his vulgar perversions and his total disrespect for females. Since I am the father of three beautiful daughters, Weezer totally disgusts me.

Old Mutha' Hubbid and "Locomotive Breath"*

For purposes of confidentiality, I have changed this big fella's name to "Old Mutha' Hubbid." Old Mutha was a very dark-skinned black and he was large! Large in the sense that he was built very thick.

Old Mutha would usually sit in my classroom and generally keep up a running commentary in his deep basso profondo voice about anything and everything that was wrong in his world. Old Mutha was just now attempting to learn how to write in cursive! On the other hand, "Locomotive Breath"* was a gangly black who was generally useless as far as undertaking his assigned class-work. *"Don't put that shit in front of me!"* Or,. "If I see you on the street someday. I will kill you!"

ME: "Don't worry, you will never, *EVER* find me anywhere near the streets that *YOU* walk!"

*(With all due respects to the classic, British rock band, **"Jethro Tull"** for their great, hard-rocking song, **"Locomotive Breath."**)*

*NOTE: See Epilogue to find out what happened to "Locomotive Breath" during the Summer of 2012.

> **'The Beast':** Lieut. Dan and I have given this nickname to a
> student inmate who almost defies description. Because student/
> inmates come and go in and out of these detention centers,
> they are known as 'Frequent Fliers'. The highly superstitious
> Lieut. Dan deeply believes that if a teacher ever utters the
> name of a discharged student out loud then that teacher has
> inadvertently summoned the student/inmate back!

The major thing I could tell you about "Locomotive Breath" is that
he had such a severe case of halitosis that his horrendous breath could
have brought a speeding locomotive to a screeching stop! Consequently,
I always tried to maintain at least a four-foot radius away from this
obnoxious and semi-crazy stinker. He was often barking out a bunch
of garbage about how bad-ass tough he was; which was sort of comical
considering his unimposing physique.

One day, "Locomotive Breath"* took it just a little too far and this
caused "Old Mutha" to pick him up and then body-slam him down onto
the hard classroom floor. It took three guards to subdue "Old Mutha"
while I tried to brave the stink and keep "Locomotive Breath" off and in
a corner until the guards could come back to remove his humiliated self
to the infirmary. "The Beast" has been in and out of this place so many
times because no other detention center, or halfway house can hold 'it'.
'The Beast' is a black, Transgender female. I will refer to 'The Beast' as
a 'her' because that is the way the facility has to classify and treat her/
him. S/he is Bi-polar, strong as a man and hostile as hell towards anybody
that is white. (Particularly white males.) The female JCOs are obviously
afraid of 'The Beast' because they are notoriously slow to act whenever
'The Beast' goes into his/her screaming and destructive acts. 'The Beast'
is real big on trashing classrooms. She has turned over numerous heavy
tables and knocked over large and loaded file cabinets two separate times
in my classroom! She will blast out primal screams and is a "cutter." Most
of the time 'The Beast' is on "No pencil status/ crayon only."

The Beast throws bits of crayons at the teachers and will pull staples
out of soft magazines or books to use to cut herself. Basically all of the
teachers agree that a Juvenile Detention Center is no place for 'The
Beast'. S/he needs to be in a mental Institution where s/he can get proper
professional help and be well away from all of the toxic characters she
interacts with in here. One day 'The Beast' was sitting close to Twinkles

and I couldn't help but overhear their conversation. As usual, Twinkles was asking all sorts of nasty questions. 'The Beast' then let go with the longest, loudest and wettest fart ever cut! BARF! Not to be denied, Twinkles was flexing that he had been sexually molested at three years old, or maybe he was telling the truth. Hard to tell with Twinkles.

The Beast is so obviously angry over the cruel joke that God had played on her/him. (What a horrible situation s/he was born into.) So sad. The mere sight of 'The Beast' entering your classroom elicits feelings of revulsion. S/he has sat her fat self down upon my desk, opened his/her eyes wide to look totally deranged and stated *"I will get you!"* 'The Beast' repeatedly *growled*, ... *"Get! Get! Get!"* with her fingers pointed towards me while twisted into some stupid gang symbolism.

Lieut. Dan's take on the Beast: *"They need to chain it in a corner and feed it with a slingshot."*

Transgender Dysphoria: (There's a lot of it Going Around!) Recently the Justice Dept. and the Georgia Dept. of Corrections have issued several policies to address ongoing assessments, evaluations, treatments and protections for inmates that are or were diagnosed with Transgender Dysphoria. This unfortunate condition can be especially problematic for all involved in residing, or working a Detention facility.

Chapter Seven

A Rogues Gallery, Continued
(Some of Those That I Truly Came To Enjoy)

Defarta: A 16 year old black who is ADHD and has major problems with flatulence.(A problem with lactose perhaps?) Defarta has cut some of the loudest, the wettest and surely the longest farts ever cut! Thus, I have tagged him with the nickname Defarta. (My term of endearment.) I like Defarta, but he sure can be a handful.He likes to sit next to my desk where he can eyeball the hallway and possibly spot the occasional female. (Air pollution! . . . Geez!) DeFarta thinks I'm a good teacher unless I ask him to do some classwork. Defarta is very observant and always asks the most direct questions:

"Mr. Kelly, Why your upper lip so thin?" or, *"Mr. Kelly you got a big head!"* And, ..."*You got wrinkles on your elbows!"* Or after patting my head, *"Why your hair so soft?"*

DeFarta would usually enter my classroom bouncing around with arms flapping and dancing the "Soljia Boy." Defarta is seemingly kind and definitely, a free spirit. I liked him.

"The Mouth": Oh brother! She just couldn't stop running her mouth from the time she enters the classroom and she is so LOUD! 'The Mouth' is a light skinned black female and quite attractive. Almost (Model quality) Everything with the (mouth) turns into major drama. All she wants to do is to write and exchange notes with the male inmates. 'The Mouth' is obviously ADHD. She stands in the classroom doorway, or in the hallway shouting out to whomever she can in order to gain attention.

While in the hallway she will pass notes and flirt with any male inmate that is in her field of vision.Getting 'The Mouth' to sit down and to become quiet always turns into a major battle.

You can't tell me where to sit! Fuck you! Don't you talk to me! I'm upset today. I'm buckin'!" Countless times 'The Mouth' has come into my classroom in tears. It's usually over a fight with another girl or its always a tragedy (Some relative died, or a detention center boyfriend had shipped out).The Mouth refuses all assigned class-work and gets even madder if I try to convince her to settle down and get started. No teacher is happy to have 'The Mouth' in his/her classroom. Lieut. Dan, in particular, has a major personality conflict with 'The Mouth'. She can hardly last five minutes in his classroom before she is sent out to AEPM! The "Big 0" would also be thrilled to see 'The Mouth' move on and out. As for me, I try to tolerate her outbursts, but she is so disruptive that I would also be perfectly happy to see her leave for good, 'The mouth' seems to tolerate me as I tolerate her. One time 'The Mouth' had been gone for an extended amount of time. It turns out that she had been pregnant, but not showing. I asked her how things had gone and she wrote down on a piece of paper,

A-B-O-R-T-I-O-N-

I quietly said to her, *"That must have been very hard on you."* And then added, *"You probably did the best thing. You probably weren't ready to look after a little baby. So don't put yourself on a big guilt trip, or let anybody else put you on a big guilt trip over this. You're abig girl and you made a very mature decision."*

Because I gave her a little empathy and support at that moment, she seems to have come around to thinking that I might just be O.K. That is, until I have to crack down on her out of control behavior the next time. And then I'll just be another "racist motherfucker."

Wilbrooks: One time Wilbrooks entered my classroom and 'sneaked' another student.("'The Mess.")They became entangled so I reached my arm under Wilbrooks' neck and lifted him up off 'The Mess." This got his feet off the floor.(He was pretty small at the time.) I then carried him out of the classroom and passed him off to a JCO. Wilbrooks is constantly fighting and he does seem to be a tough little bugger.

I asked Wilbrooks why he wants to fight so much and he said: *"I like the adrenalin rush."*

So I told Wilbrooks that when he gets back to high school he should try out for football and specifically as a strong safety. Then he would get to hit as many people as hard as he wants and still get the adrenalin rush!

Actually Wilbrooks is quite fast and quick. After returning to this facility again, he had obviously gotten bigger and stronger. One time Wilbrooks and another student had conspired to write some pretty nasty and demeaning notes to one highly disturbed young girl.(Desireé) So one day, Desiré marched right into my classroom, straight up to Wilbrooks and with a closed fist, slugged him squarely in the chops!.

A really good and forceful shot! To my amazement Wilbrooks just grinned,threw his arms around Desire' in order to constrain her. Virtually any other male in here would have probably slugged her right back, but he told me, *"I don't hit females."* *Wilbrooks* gained a lot of my respect with that statement, but he definitely did deserve to get slugged! Guess what Wilbrooks is gearing up to do as a future career? . . . Ultimate fighting! I really do like this little guy. At this writing, he can't be much more than 5'7"170 lbs. and maybe he'll have another growth spurt. I still think he'd make an excellent strong safety in football.

CeeJay: A good guy with obvious ADHD and highly verbal. Never can stop talking, He usually brings a smiling and sunny disposition into my classroom. CeeJay is a muscular black of medium size, but I've just got to share with you this one anecdote about CeeJay. One morning CeeJay entered my classroom happily dancing and singing a song that he obviously could not get out of his head. The song was "I Feel Pretty" from the Broadway musical, "West Side Story.". How incongruous was that?

Here's this macho black dude prancing and dancing around the room singing happily, *"I feel pretty, oh so pretty and witty and gay, and I pity any girl that isn't me today!"*

Believe me, CeeJay is no Natalie Wood!

Cody: What a good little guy!. Cody is a short, light-skinned Black and an excellent Basketballer. Obviously a born-to-be point guard. Cody is a super tenacious defender, slight of build, but strong enough, One day, Cody came into my classroom weeping terribly. He curled up in a corner and asked for a tissue. He was un-consolable and god only knows what might have happened overnight to cause Cody such distress.(Sexual abuse?) Cody kept answering my entreaties with,. *"I want my mamma! I want my mamma!"* Our Assistant Administrator came by, saw Cody'sdistress and me trying to console him. He went and got the dog we have here to help soothe and cool down some of the most upset inmates. Didn't work. *"No! I'm afraid of clogs!"* At this point I figured that maybe Cody needed a little tough love. I had recently been promised that I would be coaching a detention center basketball team. So I said to Cody, *"Cody you're going to be my point guard and as you know, Point guard is the most important position on the floor. The point guard is the distributor and the creator of the offense. He must be a strong leader in every way but no one is going to respect a point guard who is crying for his mamma. So you've got to grow up and be a man!"* This somehow got Cody going and from that point on, Cody and I eveloped a great relationship. He does all his work, never bucks and hardly makes a peep. Other than to come up to my desk and ask for things like, *"Ah need a tissue. Ah need a pencil. Ah need some paper, Ah need some lotion. Ah need my assignment. Give me some work."* Or, *"Mr. Kelly, ah need some sleep today."* So now Cody has earned the nickname "Ah-Need."

Cody/ "Ah-Need" had been given the reading assignment of Rudyard Kipling's classic story, 'Rikki-Tikki-Tavi'.

One of the questions Cody was asked to answer was: The animals in this story think and talk as if they were human. How do you feel about stories like this? Do you like them? Or do you prefer to read about real animals without human characteristics? Cody's written response: *"Yes, I like animals but I do not like false story. Sometimes I do, but about snakes and a mongoose I do not like."* Maybe I'll have Cody read"Animal Farm" next time!

A year passed by and Cody had gone on to another Detention center.

One day, I received a new student into my class who had been at the same Detention Center as Cody. The new student carried greetings from Cody! You know what? . . . I guess that's what doing this stuff is all about. That was so nice to hear.

Every now and then these guys can come up with some pretty funny stuff. They're not all totally hopeless. Here's what some smart-ass had written into a Physical Science textbook chapter on FORCE. Under a picture of a female ice skater, the question had been altered to read *How hard would you have to push a 240kg penis to increase her speed by 2m/sec/sec?* The miscreant had scratched out the word skater and changed it to penis! I have to admit it gave me quite a chuckle and certainly appealed to the smart-ass within me. It's funny to me because it truly reflects the never-ending mindset of all the sexually frustrated inmates that reside in here.

Chapter Eight

Notes (Student to Student)

I would pick up all sorts of forgotten or crumpled up notes at the end of each class period, or school-day. These notes might be on the floor, on a desk, inside a book, inside a student's file folder, or on a bookshelf. I include herein a few sample notes simply because they provide a little insight into these various inmates' thought processes, values, or anger. The inmates have developed the most ingenious method for folding their notes into tight little triangles of folded paper. Somehow they get word to the intended about where they might find the notes.I have typed them as I have found them. Punctuation is apparently, not necessary. Read on but I warn you, this is not easy reading and sometimes it is just filthy. Here's a sad one that was forgotten and left by Mina, one of my favorite female students:

> "These are my confessions. Just when I thought I had said everything, she said I got one on the way. These are my confessions. Damn I'm grown and I don't know what to do. I guess I have to keep part two of my confession."

About two days later Mina was visited by medical and suddenly erupted in tears of joy. She was O.K. from there on out. Not much later Mina was discharged to parts unknown. I wonder how she's doing these days. She's a good kid. I hope things will turn out and get better for her. She's got a lot going for her. Reasonably intelligent, athletic, quite attractive and seems to have a lot more common sense than most of the others have in here.

Jakeel is working on his RAP:

"Jakeel is da best rapper alive!
I'm pullin' triggas Niggas
Fall off while I'm in the streets
Niggas steady tryin 2 pop it off
Niggaz tryin 2 run up on me now they made a big mistake
Now da army comin' and they think it's a mutha fuckin earthquake I got pussy niggaz runnin scared."

Quianna, a very angry black girl left these stream of consciousness scribblings that she forgot to take with her when class ended:

"Fuck
Bitch
Stick it up ya ass nigga
Fuck the world
Fuck Paulding County fuck all them haters
Fuck Ms. O—
Fuck what those haters say
Fucking stupid ass bitches."

Derontae AKA 'Bone' a lanky black male who refuses to do any class-work. *"Don't put that shit in front of me!"* This is part of a letter to a friend on the outside that he, 'Bone', left behind: "What's up my nigga. What you been up to brah? Shid me'n just chillin off in this thang tryin make it happen. Shid I'm straight though my nigga. Let me tell you brah I was chillin in the pod yesterday when officer Doggett walked in and he was like *"Bone do you got hands?"* I was like nigga what kind of shit is that dude? So he said Look man I want you to do some for me so shid he put my ass in the room with these two niggas. Tumbo and this new dude and he told me to top his ass so shid I dove off in the shit. real talk my nigga I'm beastin in this shirt. For real dawg tell Quan I said whats up larry to. Do something for me brah tell Dasha its over real talk my nigga tell her she fouled out brah. Nai mean? But bout my time? And yeah I got 60 days and when I get out I still get 9-15 months to do. I kno they tryin hide a nigga but shid I'm about to go Rec. No homo but I love you brah u a real ass nigga dawg. I came April 28 and we gone have a smokin section light brah so be ready cause we gone kush it up dawg."

(NOTE: At this point Bone provides his MY-SPACE E-mail address).
"P.S. give it to ladreke"
Here's another letter to someone named Dwossy:

"Dear Dwossy what up? I was lock up with Welsey and they ship me off. And tell your brother Tevin said that when I get out that we are going to get fuck up. I write Jerry and Tevin and now I am write you tell them niggia that I said hold it down I get out June 19. Dwossy told me that red and them lame street nigga came and shot at Trayvon and Jay and them. I told them nigga that they didn't listen to me and when I get out I am going to beat them nigga ass. I know that I miss ZD lne day and I know y'all niggaa got fuck up. Tell Petreo I said happy birthday because I am going to miss his birthday. The city pool is about to open may 29 I will be getting out about 2 week later, And you know the 4 of july is coom up so you need a gun. Tell Bishop and Pistrol I said what up. Tell everybody I said what up and you need to go the trasp. And start traping listen to me. Be careful l'il bro.

One love
P.S. R.I.P. Donnie zo2ne boy for life."

Now, is that a stupid letter? Or what???

Chapter Nine

Ain't love great?
(students' "love" notes)

The following "love notes" are so confused and totally lacking in any kind of real understanding of achieving a meaningful and fulfilling relationship.

Tina to some unknown guy:

> *"Hey! Was up? Me shit just in class. But anyways I don't know why you want me to write you. But I did not want you to be mad at me. But I go to court on the 18th so pray I go home, but I got to go. Peace. It all go good in court I'll be good. O.K. Bye"*

Tina again this time to one of her black suiters:

> *"Hey! Was up? Me shit just chillin in class lot this shit is lame as hell. Man I miss your bad ass. But any ways why was you even in that shit? Man dogg you make me want to kill myself."*

Here's a note written to Tina:

> *"2 skittles from lil' A: I love you. Hey waz up well Im just writing to you to tell you how much I love you. And I want to go out with you but why you always get mad at me for no reason. Let me tell you something I don't like girls that be getting jealous. Well I'm going to tell you the true I be thinking of you every day and I hope*

that one day me and you can get out and talk in the outside. I hope you don't forget about me when you get out and write me or if I get out before you I'm going to write you tell your MOM to mail you a picture of you so you can give it to me. I'm going to give you my address so you can write me. Well write me back ASAP I love you." (I think that one is from De-farta but it could have been from Auzzen)

Here's one from who knows???? To whomever??? Tina??????

"Wat up. Wat u been doing? I haven't been doing nothing but thinking about you, but like I was saying in the first letter is that I won't to go with you so answer my question do you want to go with me. Oh yeah I heard something bout you to. Them bitch ass nigga you hang with tol me that the dude with the short dreads finger you in the classroom when we had group. I don't believe them, but I am asking you and you ain't got to lie to me. But anyway them nigga don't care about like I do. they just want to hit then leave you but I'm feeling you and I want to stay with you. You act like you can't talk to me when we be at meeting or something you talk to them nigga. One more thing Boneapart told me that you like him. If you do just tell me. But on some real shit I like you and write back don't write back with no two sentence either. And you didn't say happy birthday either. Yeah but write back baby."

(Hey, wait a minute! I thought Bonaparte was in exile on Elba! This poor frustrated boy is being played pretty good by The sort of un-interested and two sentence-writing Tina and he's blowin' it . . . . Damn!)

Uh oh! Here's one from 'Big daddy':

"Ay baby What's good if you get out on Monday yu better write me while I'm in here ya feel me. And ya mom don't like me I'm a good kidd I like the letter you wrote me it was funny and shit ya momz change her mind she is fucking up our planz damn. Some of the JCOs was readin the letter you wrote me today cuz it fell out of my pants and after he read it he was like who is big daddy I was like me. He was like ya girl is a freak I was like tell me about it

but yea you better write me no bull shyt I get you wet as fCK don't I? Shit I wanna kno yo wildest fantasy about me and make sure you tell detilz OK write back."

(I think some of these guys worry about bad karma if they correctly write out all the vowels for the bad words. What do you think? Funny how they're trying to be all nice and loving, but they're throwing out all of their words with a lot of threats attached. Hey! He wants "DETILZ!" Do you got that???)

Roger! Wilco! . . . . Got it!

Guess who this next one's for? If you guessed it's for that bewitching goddess Tina, you'd be right!

This one's from "The Mess"

"Hey, how ya doin? I'm great considering I'm in here. I just hate this place. It's a total hell-hole. Ya know I really like ya 'n wanna get to know ya better. Like your eyes, hair, face, figure you know you got the body of a goddess. You are just too beautiful even for me. I'd love to meet you soon. Love, your secret admirer" ('The Mess' must be thinking he's some kind of Greek God or something! Give me a break! Frankly, Tina does not have the body of a "goddess," she's short and sort of thick around the middle. But I will admit that she has a cute smile when her eyes light up. I like Tina and I also like 'The Mess'. Probably because he laughs at a lot of my lame-O jokes. 'The Mess' is closer in body style to the Pilsbury doughboy than to a Greek God. They would make for a nice couple though. Tina's just a little slow (M.I.D.?) and he's actually pretty smart. They both have pleasant personalities and I enjoyed having both of them as my students).

Chapter Ten

Messin' wit de're mindz

Just to keep my sanity I have to keep ''em off stride. So, as I said at the start, Everyone in here is flexin' including the teachers!

Them: *"Mr. Kelly, do you like Rap?"*

Me: *"You know very well that all of us white-haired, old, white guys believe that Rap is short for Crap! But I guess there is one Rap song that 1 kind of like, 'Thug In Love'."*

Them: *What???! !!???*

Me: *"'Thug In love'."*

Them*: "Who did it?"*

Me: *"Gangstallicious."*

Them: *"Whooo???!!"*

Me*: "Gangstallicious! You've never heard of Gangstallicious? He's in the hospital with a gunshot wound right now! Didn't you know that? Oh yeah, some bad-ass from Eat Dirt's crew popped a cap in him in a nightclub!"*

Them: *"Whoo????"*

Me: *"Eat Dirt! Jeez, you guys been in here too long!"*

Them: *"Oh man, You be flexin!"* And finally from the back of the room Dimany said, *"Man, you been watchin'" The Boondocks!'"*

Yup! That's straight out of Aaron McGruder's cartoon DVD "The Boondocks," that satirizes black culture.

When Dimany was being discharged, he came back to my classroom to tell me he was leaving and to "watch for. him in the papers." (He is apparently a pretty good running back at a nearby high School.) He said, *"I never had a teacher that would do stuff like that!"*

Late one Friday afternoon at the end of sixth period only three guys remained in the room. Every now and then at the very last moments of the last period of the week, I might tell a few jokes. Most are completely clean such as Flip Wilson's tale of the "Ugly baby'" But there might be slightly off-color one for the good guys. After all, we're in a prison and what these guys say and do all day long probably gives me license, in my own mind, to give them a slightly off-color comedic break. (Nothing gross.) So I told these three a semi-dirty, but truly great joke with the punch-line being 'Sahara Pipelinni' (referring to the Sahara Pipeline).

Dimsman: *"I don't get it."*

Me: *"The Sahara Desert is huge and is the largest desert in the world!"*

Dimsman: *"Huh? Where is it?* (While pointing at the huge World Map on the wall).

Me: While pointing to the Arctic Circle, *"Iceland."*

Michael: Who got the original joke and understands a little something about Geography. *"Dimsman, You are so fucking stupid!"*

A red-faced Dimsman: to both Michael and,. to me: *"Fuck you! And you!"*

Here's another little gem from Lieut. Dan: We teachers were called to a Mandatory meeting along with the security staff that was to take place in the gym. As we looked at the gym floor, Lieut. Dan sizes things up as he sees several areas with numerous mousetraps spread out and all-around the floor. He turns to me and quietly mumbles:

> *"Uh oh! Looks like a team-building exercise! Be afraid! . . . Very afraid!"*

He was right! What would I do without Lieut. Dan to keep me loose?

Chapter Eleven

This Place is Killing Me!

You know, there are so many people out there in positions of authority who can make your working hours so miserable that you can't help but wonder how in the world did this, or that no talent person ever rise up to his/her current position? That was pretty much how I would describe the daily wondering of the teachers who worked so diligently in the hell-hole that we were all working within. The Administrative/management culture was highly toxic towards the virtually all-white Education Dept. If the crazy student/inmates didn't get me first, I figured that over the long run, the management induced stress would ultimately ruin my overall health. I sensed that our facility's upper management was wary of me and perceived me to be a potentially un-manageable "whistle-blower." (This was mainly because I did not fit the normal "shrinking violet" teacher profile and had previously spent over forty years as an executive in the business world.)

Our Assistant Administrator was a wiry little white guy from Eastern Tenessee and he was one of those hardscrabble types who believed that his dictates should never be questioned. (I wouldn't have been surprised if he had been brought up by a hard and very demanding father.) On the surface he seemed quite friendly and confident. But after a while I began to notice that maybe he could be just a little insecure in himself. (Not insecure in his job, but perhaps just a little insecure in himself.) Our teaching staff was constantly made to feel that we were not highly valued and that we could be let go at any time. Our Assistant Administrator would repeatedly tell us that *"If you don't like it here, you can always quit.* " Yearly reviews were sort of a farce. *Our Assistant Administrator employed a four point rating system. He would nit-pick over the smallest things. A score of four in any category was virtually impossible to achieve. An overall three rating worked out to be, "meets expectations." I guess he didn't want anybody to think that they were outstanding, or even indispensable. Every single teacher always got the identical "Gotcha" comment which went something like this. "I often look into your classroom and it seems as if you're not fully aware of everything that's going on." (This oft-repeated phrase was clearly designed to protect the company in the case of a serious incident and would definitely hang the poor teacher out to dry.)* There was one particular teacher that Our Assistant Administrator clearly didn't care for and he decided to run her off by some horrendously unprofessional comments such as,... *"I don't think you are even fit to flip burgers at a MacDonalds."*

Sometimes during lunch hour our Assistant Administrator would sneak around the school's hallways in an attempt to find teachers eating their lunches together. He always insisted upon what he called "working lunches." Had I been the Assistant Administrator in this hell-hole, I would have strongly urged my teaching staff to socialize, share info and vent to each other. After all our jobs were the most stressful, dangerous and frustrating imaginable. One time during a lunch-time staff meeting he really got into it with our Education Department's primary record-keeper. She was a grey-haired, middle-aged woman who could get pretty outspoken whenever she felt that we were all getting the short-end. He jumped up, stamped his foot, slammed clown his papers and clipboard onto the floor, hitched his pants up and screamed *"I'm so darned sick of this! You can quit anytime you want!"* And she barked back, *"Fine, 1 quit!"* And the momentarily stunned education staff quietly watched this train wreck unfold before our disbelieving eyes. After the dust had settled and the combatants had left the room, good old Lieut. Dan came up with a beaut. Popping his eyes wide open like a worried little kid he said, *"Mommy and daddy are fighting . . . I'm scared!"* An interesting observation about this little banty rooster of a man, was how he always hitched his pants and stomped his foot whenever he got mad, or upset. Several times when I had challenged him for the way he was ripping me over the most inconsequential things. He would hitch up the pants, stomp his foot and scream, *"Stop that! Stop that right now!"*

(See my not-too-great caricature on this page). Actually, the caricature must be pretty good because at a DJJ. sponsored Education Seminar, I showed it to another Special Ed teacher who used to work at our facility. She laughed and recognized him right away!

Chapter Twelve

Just a Few More 'Love' Notes

Here's just four more. This first one is from Auzzen. Remember the slimy skulker? You will note that Auzzen is not much on punctuation. In this note Auzzen seems to be trying out his chops in providing sexual advice:

"Wuz a me not much just thinking about the first letter you ever wrote to me I tried to remember what all it said all I remember is you said that you liked it in 69 different positions. That the way a lot of people are. but I'm ready whenever you are. The only reason I was talking to Drf was because I want her to let me fuck her, but I don't Guess she wants me to because I touched her today and she got mad. I don't really care anymore because I don't think she does. Tell her to write me if she does or, is she hate me. I wasn't trying to harm myself last night I just won't to get them to open my door that's all so baby just chill and write me back 5th period OK."

Sometimes a male and female student will get together to play a little game of writing comments to each other on a piece of paper that they pass back and forth.

Here's beaut! A new form of 'Dear John letter' (Prison-style).

Female: "I don't like your attitude and you talking about you can beat my ass. That not cool. So you would hit a girl. And I am not scared of you but that's cool. And you right I can't tell you what to do."

Male: "I was just playin. I would not hit a girl I just wanting to talk to you."

Female: "Man, whatever, I am about to get out in 2 day. I don't need no relationship in RYDC so you know what that means."

Male: "I've been know dat I'm gone leave you alone."

Female: "Yes that's what I want thank you. Don't talk to me no more and I never wanted to go out with you that's why I was acting like that. You too big for me and when you talking about given me some dick. No thank you. and I don't care if you want to lick me up and down I will never let you put your lips or your tongue in me."

Male: "You asked me out so fuck it I am gone. Bye bye."

(Comment: I guess he somehow preserved what little manhood he had left with that last shot!)

Every now and then someone will surprise you. Michael came up with this little gem on Valentine's Day:

> "Hey beautiful! I didn't get to read the last letter you wrote because Lalina can't pass notes to save her life. Anyways I still don't know your name. Ms.Sh_ _li (A J.C.O.) said it was M . . . . . th. I wanna know more about you, because you're a beautiful face in a bad place and I wanna know why? HAPPY VALENTINE'S DAY! And she really is a beautiful face! Good job Michael!

Now here's an overly long and confusing mess from Chriz, a very confused SEBD and ADHD young man who is half white and half black. This note is quite nasty, but it clearly demonstrates how all the tangled circuits in these impaired brains are so jumbled-up and seemed to have shorted out. I have done my very best to translate what was nearly an unreadable effort, so bear with me:

> "2 baby girl
>
> 4rm baby boy reason: let u know wats good mama I'm started off like this I already knew about you an that nigga you was with when I came over. because you told me dat you smoke

some weed with him an I already know about you because that's what a nigga do he smoke with her an he fuck because dats why I was callin you a freak all the time. Come on now but I didn't know you fuck nigga in the a, but I should have knew because you stupid you tell me that he ain't like dat. You fuck yourself up you digg if I was there for you why would you do that to me I don't understand why yea digg. An you say I put it down. Yo get real." . . . .

(*NOTE:* At this point I had to remove two totally confused paragraphs as barely readable. Here's the Grande Finale:

. . . "Look I knew you was doin your thing so I did my thing digg but stayed faithful 2 for a longtime . . . when you ask me will I always be there for you and I said yea that's when I broke up with my baby mama. I left her for you an you fuck these niggas you don't even know like dats a freak. Real shit these niggas don't smoke wit you because you cool to chill wit because you don't think when you high. Real shit. But you to young to know that you better open your fuckin eyes. Baby girl these niggas ain't got know fuck love for you like I do. Real shit take it from somebody that know because when you get high you wet. I know just like when my brother an me an you was walkin an you grab me all over an shit you just don't know how I feel as I am readin this shit . . . But you can take that shit back so fuck it yea digg Baby pray that things would not change. I should let you keep it to yourself but good you didn't lie to me. An you fuck a nigga in a group home you don't know these niggas an you just fuckin off bad. I don't know I want to have sex wit you right now hell no I don't play dat shit fool around and catch HIV an don't pass it you to me then. An yea I love you with all my heart. You is still my baby mama baby an no I will not change when I get out you don't want to know how many girl I been with since we been to there. A lot! Just to get back at you. but still love you baby. Yes I do. I want to have a baby by you. When we did it I nutted in you like four times but you didn't blow up. but I want you to be my baby and don't have 30 girls but its close. I don't go out wit them but we talkin. Yea digg I hope to answer all your questions mama.

Oh I give that girl your letter today an when I in the gym Ms. C had it. yo tell her I said fuck her for doin that She ain't your friend. Lame ass. Love you."

WHEWW! Ain't love great?? I think I need a bath!

As Lieut. Dan, my next door guru, summed it up: *"These guys would try to make love to a knot hole!"*

Chapter Thirteen

The State of Public Education

After the ***"No Child Left Behind Act"*** became Public Education Policy, Public Education in the Deep South, and particularly in Georgia, can best be described these days as a ***"Hot Mess."*** (Inadequate funding, over-crowded classrooms, Administrators' requiring teachers to alter and correct wrong answers on the recording of CRCT Test answers, etc.!)

You can't do a darned thing about quality of parenting, or negative environmental influences. Obviously it's the schools in upper middle, or middle class neighborhoods that consistently rate near the top of school ratings lists. Demographic statistics provide empirical evidence for this. This is all so obvious that there is no need for further discussion. If the families, or the community values higher education, the students receive encouragement, reading assistance and homework support. If there is a toxic community culture that denigrates higher education, or authority, the result is low performance and a high rate of addictions, school dropouts and criminality. Consideration of such obvious demographics must always be a major part of a school's or a teacher's performance ratings. Is it all about quality of teachers? Sort of. Most studies cite the importance of the teacher as the 'key ingredient' in student success. Truly great teachers are pretty rare and mediocre teachers are far too prevalent. Does a long string of academic degrees make for a truly "great" teacher? I'm not so sure. But on the other hand, I would submit that this also reflects a high level of commitment to being the best one can be.Certainly such academic achievement probably makes for a good teacher. But does that make for a 'Great Leader'? I doubt it. You're either blessed with, or have learned, solid leadership skills, or you're not. I strongly believe THAT. Yet who else but a teacher is a 'leader'? Leadership skills are critically important. Without really good leadership skills, a teacher will have all sorts of problems with classroom management and with motivating his/her students to get with the program. If you're a great Leader, you will probably be a great teacher.

But if the students don't like you, or respect you, they will not be ready to learn. I often wonder, how many teachers got into teaching just so they could coach a sport? (A lot of bad ones! That's for sure.)

But wait a minute, does this make for a bad teacher? NO! Not at all! Unfortunately, however, most of us can all remember our high school classes with a stereotypical coach/teacher who was un-inspiring and more interested in just going through the motions. Perhaps throughout half of each class, s/he was drawing up plays, lineups, defenses, etc. It happens. Unfortunately these less than impressive teacher types are what gives teaching such a bad rap. And what about these sexually-driven idiots who end up getting caught messing around with one of their students? It happens far too often. I venture to say it is mostly those teachers that are under forty who can't resist the unbelievably flirtatious and attractive students that send all sorts of signals. I don't know how a hiring authority can winnow out all of the un-thinking losers who have so little self-control. Now dear reader, please understand the following. It is not just in education that such jerks exist. There are losers everywhere and sometimes, in positions of authority. They're not all in education. They are in business, in government, the military, you name it. Such "Losers" create so many problems that they create a wide readership for those of us who appreciate organization-based cartoons like 'Dilbert', etc.

Following is my own personal take on 'Leadership'. And right behind that is a listing of all the personal attributes, or key factors that I strongly believe are normally present within the "Teacher Superstar." Finally, The "No-Child Left Behind Act while necessary at the time, has probably created at least as many problems as it has solved. Is Severe Emotional Behavior Disorder a true 'Disability'? Or is SEBD just a fancy term for an extremely angry kid who needs loving attention at home. The child probably needs a small dose of "Tough love." Or how about Attention Deficit Hyperactivity Disorder?(ADHD). Is that really a disability, or Just a reflection of a non-motivated and highly immature kid who needs a chance to be in a class with other such types?

I would submit that such ADHD students are highly disruptive forces in classrooms with more highly motivated achievers who just want things to calm down and to be left alone. Furthermore, the ADHDs are particularly disruptive to those students diagnosed as ADD.

I'm a big believer in creating special facilities on school campuses that would accommodate all of the "physically disabled" students. Perhaps they might walk to the new wing, or new building, or along a different hall to get to their classes.These special facililies would, of course be able to accommodate the physically disabled with wider doorways, ramps,elevators, signage etc. and would be staffed with extra Special Ed. teachers, Parapros and even "Student Volunteers." The 'Special Needs" students would still be able to participate with the rest of the student population in school activities such as Band, Athletics, choir and drama etc.

But please keep the major classroom "disrupters" the [ADHDs] apart from the others until the "disrupters" can "earn" their way back into the regular student population classrooms.

And like the Mildly Intellectualy Disabled, Forrest Gump so famously said, . . ."And thayat's all I have to say about thayat!"

Quality of Education in Juvenile Detention Centers:

A recent page one article in the March 1, 2014 issue of the Atlanta Journal/Constitution cited the poor academic performance of Georgia's Juvenile Detention Center inmates. The article noted that "four out of five" of the tested failed their "End of Course Tests" in Biology, Math and Social Studies. It's a disturbing article and it should be read. However, as long as these Detention Centers are allowed to function "on the cheap," without a guard (JCO) presence in each classroom, chaos and failure will reign.

Unfortunately, two or three DJJ schooled students were quoted in the article typically placing blame for their failure to learn on every single thing, or everyone else they could blame,… **Other than themselves!** It is sad, but not surprising considering that it was the circumstances from their own criminal activities that had necessarily placed them into juvenile detention. These two or three "students" who were quoted in the article were trying to portray themselves as innocent little angels when in reality, they were probably the most disruptive, or at best, not willing to seriously apply themselves in the classroom. From the things they said I can't help but surmise that they might have been placed into "Special Ed" classrooms as opposed to General Ed classrooms. So go ahead and blame the system, blame the teachers and blame the other inmates for your own academic shortcomings.) I just don't buy it. (It's just another example of what Lieut. Dan had so perfectly defined as "JPS Syndrome.")

Chapter Fourteen

Hidden Talents
(Drawings and Creative Writings)

I am a reasonably accomplished artist and some sort of a frustrated creative writer. Consequently, I can really appreciate the occasional spark of hidden talent that would occasionally flare up amongst my students. I majored in Fine Arts while earning my first college degree from Colgate University. At the time, I didn't know whether I would join my father in his Architecture practice, or go on to medical school to pursue a degree in Medical Illustration.

Right here and now, I'll give our Assistant Administrator some "props' for giving me a chance to teach a drawing class during the last period on Fridays. Of course I had to personally supply all of the drawing pads and colored pencils.The idea behind all of this was to use this drawing class as a motivational tool. Only students who were trying to behave during regular classes and making reasonable CAP progress would be allowed into the drawing class. But once in, they had to behave or else they were O-U-T!

Many students wanted in. Was it because one female (Tina) was in the class? Unfortunately, very few students could handle the freedom of being in such a non-academic environment. Twinkles and Darius soon "fouled-out" and were quickly gone. (I was a little sad about Darius' inability to handle this freedom because he had shown a real talent for high detail drawing.) But four students hung in there and did really well. (Tina, Cody/ "Ah-Need", Josh and Jordan.)

Jordan, in particular, demonstrated a real gift! (See the drawing of the Male Lion.) You have already met and learned a little bit about Tina and Cody "Ah-Need" within this little book, but these four were really into participating.

The drawing students started out with basic still life drawing of objects such as apples, oranges, bananas, etc. They would work on shading and perspective. As the students progressed, I would provide them with several Art magazines that were available for any student to try to copy from. They could choose some other artist's painting, or copy a painting from "Wildlife Art," Or from "Southwestern Art," or they might copy from "National Geographic" Photos, etc. After awhile, a few started out just tracing certain of the simpler selections. They would then fill-in and try to provide a sense of shading, or a third dimension, or perhaps, they might just change the choice of color. Whatever they wanted to do was O.K. by me.

As their works became completed, I would get extra color photocopies made so that two copies of the same effort could be glued back-to-back and then professionally matted. I would then tape the finished products to the inside of my classroom's hallway windows. In doing this, I was able to display their work to all the passersby outside in the hallway and also to all of the students in my classroom. Once a student was discharged I tried to make sure that they took their finished drawings with them. One day Jordan produced an incredible free-hand drawing of a male lion. He had definitely **not** traced any of it. Jordan's drawing just blew me away. (I wondered if I could have done half as well!) The drawing included herein is from a very poor photocopy that was left over after Jordan left. It doesn't do his original effort justice. Copies of Jordan's Male Lion effort always retained a place of honor in my classroom window displays. Tina and Josh remained particularly diligent in pursuing their modest drawing efforts. Cody/ "Ah-Need" started out with a tracing of a wonderful painting of a little black girl sitting on a tree stump. Everyone seemed to particularly like this one. The following page #82, includes copies of all four students' efforts. I hope you enjoy them.

Another area of hidden talent is in creative writing. Sometimes students would try to write their own RAPs, poems, or just some imagined lyrics to a future song of heir own. As I have read some of these creative writing efforts that were so proudly presented to me, I realized that even though so many of these characters might be major losers or guilty of some pretty serious crimes, they can still be harboring deep feelings that need an opportunity to come out. Since I was teaching Lit/Comp. and Language Arts to many of my students, I made every effort to allow them to pursue their own creative writing efforts. (CAPS be damned). In fact, as a favor for their good behavior, I even took a few of their efforts home with me, re-typed them and provided a little re-editing. I even placed a copyright symbol at the top! They especially liked this little touch. I have included a few efforts herein, but have had to remove the author's real names.

Do you know what "Free-Stylin'" is?

I certainly didn't until La Tozzi became a regular in some of my classes. "Free-stylin'" is rap-style, rapid fire talking in rhyme that is not written down, but merely emanates from the brain. The uncanny use of vocabulary is a major part of "free-stylin'" and for my money, La Tozzi is a Grand Master! La Tozzi was certainly gifted with verbal intelligence. I would sometimes give him a topic and he would just take-off. It all came out fresh and original! . . . Amazing! was La Tozzi another "Rain Man?"

While listening to La Tozzi winging it, all I could think of was where in the world did he ever get this large vocabulary that he uses so correctly? Absolutely amazing or even, spooky!

Chapter Fifteen

Hoop Dreams

One of the things I was promised when I first started teaching at the detention center was that I would be coaching a detention center basketball team. I decided that My point guard was going to be Cody "Ah-Need," Cody was clearly everything a coach could ever want in a point guard.There was plenty of additional talent, amongst whom there was one particular standout. For the purpose of maintaining confidentiality I will nickname him "Mondo" Greez-um.

I really liked "Mondo'" and to these eyes he was clearly a special basketball talent. So special, in fact, that I told him one day that I felt he was clearly a division1 college talent. I visualized 'Mondo' as a shooting guard. I further emphasized that nobody would ever see his talent as long as he was languishing in a detention center. In other words,he would have to move forward in his high school education,pass some standardized tests and then, and only then, could he be noticed while excelling in High School Basketball. "Mondo" was so special that I even considered contacting the Atlanta Hawks to send a scout to check him out. "Mondo" was athletically gifted and close to 6'5"or 6' 6" tall. He was an excellent shooter, court savvy and he had the "total game."

One weekend there was an in-house three-on-three basketball tournament that every detention center employee and other inmates came to watch. Since I had previously refereed youth basketball and therefore owned referee's attire(whistle, striped shirt, black pants and shoes) I volunteered to referee the tournament. I felt that the presence of a real referee made the games just that more meaningful and official.

One time, while teaching in my classroom, I dropped my pencil on the floor and bent over to pick it up. While doing so, 'Mondo' barked out *"Hey get your ass out of my face!"* and, before I knew it, I had barked right back *"Well get your face out off my ass"*. My totally inappropriate spur-of the-moment retort instantly drew a huge amount of laughter and guffaws. Oh well, I guess such an inappropriate retort can so easily happen in such a depraved and gritty atmosphere.It had all rubbed off on me. (Can't do that in a public school!)

But, before I knew it had happened, 'Mondo' was shipped out and had disappeared into Georgia's Juvenile Detention System (probably somewhere closer to his home). I never got to say goodbye. Sad and also sad for both 'The Mouth' and the little bewitching Tina, who obviously had a thing going on for the dashing "Mondo", who clearly perceived himself to be THE Alpha stud. The detention center Administration, clearly did not have the vision or the courage to support a detention center team to compete against other Atlanta area detention center teams. I had it all figured out in terms of manpower,number of guards needed and travel needs in terms of proceeding in a low-cost fashion with adequate security. But I was totally put down and discouraged from proceeding any further with my vision.

Recently an article entitled "Teaching Kids The Crossover" appeared in the "Point After" Section of the November 15, 2010 issue of "Sports Illustrated" magazine. (Page #72). Look it up: It's pretty good and inspirational!

I would often pass by the gym and watch the inmates playing basketball. I usually told them that with the exception of Mondo, very few of them had any real shooting skills. They didn't like that, but it was true. And then of course I could not resist telling them that back in the day . . . I could dunk!! Of course they didn't believe me, but I told them that I could and would prove it! Of course I couldn't do it on THAT day . . . NOT anymore and certainly not now at my current age. The next day I brought in some photographs from my glory days back in 1956 as Co-Captain of the Vermont Academy Basketball team.(See facing page.) They were totally amazed and especially amused by the shortness of my shorts and my Converse "Chucks." (The iconic Chuck Taylor Basketball sneakers by Converse.) This particular photo of me was a result of a special "Picture Day." Did I say earlier in this book that everyone in dis place is flexin'? . . . Includin' da teachers? Well, the fact of the matter is that actually . . . I jumped off of a chair for this totally posed bit of flexin'!!!

Chapter Sixteen

The End of the Pipeline

So many of the students/inmates have hardly anywhere to go after being discharged from juvenile detention. Depending upon the severity of their crimes, if they are over seventeen, they might go directly to 'Big Boys' prison. Perhaps their family situation has been found to be so toxic that DFACS (Dept. of Family and Child Services) cannot allow them back to their own families. So what to do with these poor lost souls? Usually it is directly into foster care as a ward-of-the-state, or into a so-called Group-Home. Here in Georgia the local newspaper, the Atlanta Journal/Constitution has recently completed a major expose of the unacceptable state of foster care in Georgia. Apparently the female residents in a large group home for females had gone for many days without their medicines or without proper medical supervision (the nurse had quit), The inevitable result; a major riot broke out with all sorts of fights and major property destruction. According to the AJC: "It took more than two dozen sheriffs deputies and State troopers to quell the disturbance." I just had to chuckle when I read the quote from one officer, who had spent numerous years in the military and in law enforcement and had never *"heard as much foul language used and abusive actions taken by anyone, much less young females."* (Hey Bubba . . . sounds just like I heard every single day in the detention center!)

In conclusion, the sad facts are that at the end of The Pipeline the light may well be a locomotive. Foster care remains a very dangerous option for so many juveniles, because they are constantly being exposed to violence, sexual abuse, improper medical care and other horrors, primarily because there is very little oversight and a major lack of adequate security in the larger group homes.

Epilogue

As I wrote this book my moods would constantly shift. Some days 1 was just too down to keep writing, because I was always searching for a little humor and trying for a few laughs here and there while trying to retain the reader's interest. I started to feel that my dark moods could ultimately hinder the appeal of this book.Unfortunately my work at the RYDC ended in the most ignominious fashion imaginable.

One afternoon, late in the school day, (Sixth period) the "Big O" had to leave for a dental appointment. As usually happened in the Special Ed. Dept., Lieut. Dan and 1 were given two students apiece from the 'Big O's sixth period class. I already had four regularly scheduled students of my own and these additional two new ones had not been in my class before.I only knew a little about each of them from their I.E.P.s. One, a 13 year-old and basically un-attractive, redneck female, vas obviously a very disturbed child. The other was an angry 17 year old black male.As the class priod started, several of my regularly scheduled students started to engage the new female in all sorts of ugly sex talk. She was very much the primary instigator as anyone.

Two of my previous third period students who had previously asked to have a discussion about what it would take for them to get into college, had been told to hold on until they returned for the sixth period. Midway through the sixth period, I accommodated these two and moved away from my desk area to a far corner of the room closer to one of these regular student's desk. The newly-assigned female,who had brought no math assignments with her, was given a "Far Side" cartoon book to keep her quiet and occupied. The seventeen year-old male student,who had accompanied her into my classroom, was given several "National Geographic" magazines to keep him quietly occupied. The two new students were placed in the far corner of my classroom. When I moved away from my desk area to be closer to the college interested students from 3d period. I sat down in a vacant desk which was directly under the fish-eye video camera that recorded everything that was going on in my classroom. Once I started to engage the college-interested students, the other four regular students moved over to directly in front of me while stating that they also "wanted to hear this."

Unfortunately for me, what they really wanted to do was to distract me and to screen my view of the classroom. Therefore, I could not see the female remove herself over to the far corner to be with the newly-added male student. This was all well documented in an official D.J.J., investigation that included interviews with all parties present during the "incident."

It was finally concluded that this was a self-admitted conspiracy by a group of felons to distract me and to block my view. The female student/inmate performed her oral sex act all on her own. Nobody forced her. Although I could not see it happening, I was later able to view a tape from the classroom video of her sliding herself over to the newly assigned male. Once there she proceeded to make Linda Lovelace, of "Deep Throat" notoriety look like an amateur by providing a few moments of vigorous and enthusiastic oral sex.

The next day I was placed on 'Suspension without pay' and it then took nearly three more months to finally terminate me. I was made to twist in the wind for ninety days not knowing my ultimate fate. I guess my employer, **Youth Services International** saved a lot on my teacher salary and thus delayed having to contribute to un-employment. Of course Our Assistant Administrator, never made any kind of meaningful effort to retain me. I was never given the option of resigning. He just lied and lied whenever I called to enquire after my status. (Flexin' in Hell!!) Even though I was one of his supposedly, "five *best teachers!*" (He let that slip out to me one day in a moment of weakness!) I guess he didn't really care for my occasional resistance to his management style. In fact, my "whistle-blowing" documentation, as previously mentioned, had certainly made me expendable in the eyes of The Administration.

Every day now I read the local Atlanta/Journal/Constitution to see if I recognize any of the names of any of my former students murdered, dead or captured for one more heinous crime. But here's the worst one yet!

One evening I was watching the news on TV and a young man was reported to have assaulted his grandmother with a sword. It was reported that when he was captured, "he had a Mouthful of feces!" The pictured swordsman was clearly, "Locomotive Breath!" Now "Locomotive's" horrendous halitosis finally made sense!

I later on learned that 'The Beast' had totally trashed Lieut. Dan's classroom by turning over his desk, a table and three file cabinets. Lieut. Dan was unhurt. I also heard that little 'Desireé' totally lost it and physically assaulted the female Special Ed. Teacher, who had recently replaced me. Twinkles, Claudius, Tina Cody/Ah-Need, Darius and "The Mouth" have all been long gone, but good old Willbrooks came back again! I guess Weezer is probably pissing n a corner of his Cell somewhere,or in the 'Big O's classroom.

The free-styling La Tozzi, who had been one of the two students interested in college and one of the five, who had blocked my view, was quickly removed due to results of the DJJ investigation.

Today La Tozzi is probably having a great time free-styling somewhere in another detention center on the subject of sex acts in good old Mr. Kelly's classroom.

Recently the Paulding Detention Center's designation was changed from Regional Youth Detention center (RYDC)to the generally smaller, Youth Detention Center. (YDC) And the Paulding YDC no longer houses female inmates! These two changes must have inevitably resulted in a drop in the head count along with a concurrent staff reduction. The "Big O" is gone and happily chilling out at home. Lieut. Dan is long gone after he moved out to the west coast! The elimination of female inmates was probably a good decision because too many sexual "incidents" and distractions were always occurring based upon excessive note-passing and the male inmates' prevailing need to show-off by constantly scuffling and generally playing, what I call "Grab-Ass."

After having been gone from the Paulding RYDC for nearly two years, I actually discovered that I sort of missed some of those student/ inmates, who have been described in this book; even the worst ones! Most of them were just "victims" of having been dealt a "Deadman's Hand'" at birth which placed many of them into dysfunctional and twisted family circumstances. They are fully capable of overcoming their circumstances and turning their lives around but they will still have to realize that it is they that have to do it for themselves.

Finally, if I come off sounding particularly bitter regarding the YSI Administration, ... I am. I just couldn't respect them and resented the fact that their style of leadership had created such a highly toxic and negative working environment within a facility that was already a miserable place to work. Unfortunately, the leadership culture only made matters worse for almost everyone that had to work in that godforsaken place.(It didn't need to be THAT way.)

> As someone who teaches "Leadership Skills" as a Corporate Trainer and Consultant, I can't help but feel that I must document their personal leadership shortcomings in the roles that they held . . . .

> The following news expose' reported below, resulted in the Administrator's termination along with a large number of the facility's security staff including Ibukaba. (I wonder if officer Bristlesbutt was found out and there was also one particularly effeminate JCO (R.J.) who I personally could not stand. He was, I am sure, secretly "On the down low."

> Hopefully the big broom swept him out the door along with the security staff's sexual predators. I'm not saying that he was actually gay, but my "Gaydar" *sure did cause me to suspect that he might have been a "wide receiver."*

> On **07/09/13** a major expose' Written by Staff Writer, Rhonda Cook, appeared in the Atlanta Journal Constitution:

> **"Juvenile Facility's troubles not new." "Staff, Youth sex abuse faced by management company"** "the Georgia youth Detention Center with the country's highest proportion of reported claims of sexual contact between juveniles and staff is managed by a private company with a troubled history in other states. **Youth Services International, Inc.** has had a state contract to staff and manage the **Paulding RYDC** in Dallas, west of Atlanta, since 2008 and that agreement has been renewed every year since.

> **YSI** also operates two other Georgia Youth Detention facilities . . . . last month the U.S. Department of justice released findings from a 2012 anonymous survey required by the Prison rape elimination act of 2003 that **32.1 percent** of

the juveniles at the **Paulding Center** reported inappropriate
sexual contact with staff as well as other teenagers.

**Paulding's numbers were more than three times the national
rate of 9.5 percent and were the nation's highest!"** the article goes on
to say . . . *"YSI had a "bottom-line" corporate culture that undermined
rehabilitation . . . What we see is less (staff) training, less (staff) support
and less accountability because these things are not necessarily consistent with
higher profits." NOTE: After this devastating report "The State of Georgia
closed down the Paulding RYDC and YSI terminated all of their employees
working there.*

My Treatise on Leadership

1. Great Leaders consistently Grant RESPECT to all those that they lead.
2. Great Leaders EARN respect by their ACTIONS not just their words.
3. Great Leaders are HONEST and TRUSTWORTHY. They meet their commitments and act from a deeply ingrained *value system* that provides a strong *moral compass* to guide them in difficult and morally challenging situations.
4. Great Leaders *Set the Example.* They ask no more of others than they would do themselves. They are willing to take on the most difficult and least enjoyable task. They demonstrate to others that such mundane tasks are often Important and that the *leader* will do whatever is necessary to achieve a successful result. (No task is beneath them).
5. Great Leaders must be excellent COMMUNICATORS. Their words can inspire, when delivered clearly and with charisma. They can easily explain the *why.*
6. Great Leaders are also good LISTENERS. They accept and welcome frank and open counsel even when it may disagree or run counter to the leader's pre-conceived convictions.
7. Great Leaders are ENTHUSIASTIC, ENCOURAGING and POSITIVELY Minded. No challenge is ever too great.
8. Great Leaders exhibit a strong and vibrant **"Presence."** This *presence* stems from confidence and the way they carry themselves. (voice, body language and decisiveness all combine to create "*presence').*
9. Great Leaders ***anticipate.*** They see what could or might go wrong in advance.

10. Great Leaders really do **CARE.** This is very important. The leader's caring *attitude* is instinctively recognized by those being led.

11. Great Leaders possess **GOOD JUDGEMENT.** Common sense and flexibility are constants). A truly 'great' leader can admit that he/she can be wrong and readily accepts the good and workable suggestions from those that they supervise.

12. Great Leaders treat those they lead with **FAIRNESS** and **EQUALITY** and do not prejudge. Great Leaders recognize that there is a subtle difference between treating people *fairly* and *equally.*

13. Great Leaders **DEMAND RESULTS.** They know they can expect to receive only that which they DEMAND. They realize that the normal human being will always look for *shortcuts* and attempt to avoid otherwise difficult tasks. The great LEADER consistently enforces his/her DEMANDS through *consequences* and swiftly follows through in enforcing *consequences.*

14. Leadership is a lonely place. Many times the "Leader" must make the hard decisions. The Great Leader willingly makes the *hard decisions* (The BEST decision may not always be the most *popular* decision). Great Leaders always know when to *do "the right thing".*

15. Great Leaders want to earn **RESPECT** but also appreciate friendship, if it develops. Friendship only happens as a result of consistent and positive leadership. Ultimately good RESULTS are what counts more than anything. Friendship is simply the surprisingly pleasant by-product of a successful Leadership role.

16. Great Leaders have enough self-confidence to readily *accept the blame* when things go wrong.

"It was my fault, all my fault. Now you must help me,"

(General Robert E. Lee meeting the retreating remnants of Pickett's Brigade at the Battle of Gettysburg immediately after the disastrous *Pickett's Charge)*

My Treatise On Hiring the "SuperStar" Teacher:

Given the fact that a teacher "candidate" must have mastered Course Content and enough pedagogy to be considered "Professional," there are ten (10) Critical Personal Factors/Characteristics that must be present within the Teacher candidate for the candidate to have the potential to ultimately become a Teaching "Superstar" or, to be a strong candidate for "Teacher of the Year."

What are these ten Personal Factors/Characteristics?

1. ***Brains/Intelligence:*** The very best Teachers are usually extremely intelligent. High intelligence allows them to 'think on their feet', to be creative in problem-solving and probably causes them to be more curious about the subject they teach. High intelligence allows the teacher to rapidly grasp new concepts and to rapidly master new technology. Great teachers are usually extremely intelligent.

2. ***Interpersonal People Skills:*** A warmth of personality and true enjoyment from interacting positively with other human beings is important. The ability to 'read' people(E.Q.) is a gift that few possess in abundance. Along with that warmth of personality comes a sense of humor (preferably non-sarcastic). This is the ability to laugh often at oneself, at things that happen and readily share a laugh with others. Along with a good sense of humor there is usually a strong sense of fun.

3. ***Verbal & Written Skills:*** The ability to take a complex thought, or subject and to simplify it into easy-to-understand concepts for the students, is the essence of great teaching. Teaching is

fundamentally about the art of communication. However, good communication skills are also critically needed beyond the classroom, whenever communicating up-line to administration, parents or other staff members.

4. *Presentation Skills:* This is that unique ability to project forcefully and interestingly to an entire classroom. It requires the ability to allow students to hear, see and possibly to do. The voice must be strong, pacing must be upbeat and voice tone must change. The effective use of supporting and appropriate Audio/Visual Aids can add immeasurably to a successful lesson. It is in this ability to effectively "present" that the great teacher allows his/her true personality to come out. Interesting presentations actively INVOLVE the audience.

5. *Creativity:* Creativity is a big factor' in successful problem-solving but it is also critically important in devising methods to create Class Interest in the lesson being given.

6. *Leadership:* A Superior Teacher not only manages a classroom but they also "lead" their classes to success. Leadership implies the ability to inspire people to action. Leadership, like Respect, must be earned.

7. *Responsibility & Judgement:* What is appropriate? What is Professional? What is "The Right Thing"? Teachers are afforded a huge measure of trust and they must never betray the "Sacred Trust," that is implied at all times. The Community, the School Board, the Administration, faculty, parents and even students all expect and demand that teachers be responsible and always exercise good judgement in everything they do.

8. *Sense of fairness:* Both students and their parents are acutely attuned to a sense of whether the teacher is Fair. If the teacher is not always and consistently fair, then S/He will ultimately lose respct, and worse, lose control.

9. *Organization/Planning:* Lessons must have a purpose and a goal. The entire school year must have an overall Strategic Plan, that comprehends the year-long goals. Such plans can be broken down month-to-month, week-to-week and even down to day-to-day. Teaching is a profession with a plague of Paperwork. The person who lacks interest in Planning will probably be unhappy and will struggle.

10. ?????: Finally, last, but not least, there is one other critical component that will always be Present within the Teacher 'Superstar'. That final factor is:

Teacher "SuperStars"_absolutely_and_without_hesitation,_LOVE their_jobs! If the teacher candidate doesn't, then something is seriously wrong. Either they have lost class respect, or they have lost classroom control,or they have not responded positively to the functions demanded of them by the school's administration, or by the parental community.

"BAD" Teachers lack all ten of these Personal Factors.

"POOR" Teachers lack most of these Personal Factors or possess them only in limited degrees.

"GOOD" Teachers possess most of these Personal Factors but might be slightly high or slightly weak in certain categories. They are still effective and may get the job done satisfactorily.

"GREAT TEACHERS" possess every single one of these Personal Factors in abundance.

The following is a quotation from an article by Jonathan Alter in the November 6th 2010 issue of Newsweek Magazine. In this article titled, **"A Case of Senioritis,"** Jonathan Alter refers to Microsoft founder, Bill Gates, whose immersion into studying the problems within America's public schools' pay structures, which primarily reward seniority, are probably one of the largest factors in creating low school system performance.

"Seniority is the two-headed monster of education—it's expensive and harmful. Like Masters Degrees for teachers, *"seniority pay has little correlation to student achievement."* Gates says.

After exhaustive study, the Gates Foundation and other experts have learned that the only in-school factor that fully correlates is quality teaching, which seniority hardly guarantees. Gates favors a system where pay and promotion are determined not just by improvement in test scores but by peer surveys, student feedback (surprisingly predictive of success in the classroom), video reviews and evaluation by superiors."

I am so pleased that I seem to be thinking along the same lines as someone so brilliant as Bill Gates. The only difference that I can see between Mr. Gates's observations and mine is that I also emphasize parental evaluations. This is because I believe that the parents always know who the really good teachers are. Furthermore many of the Higher paid teachers have what I call "Decorative" Masters Degrees. Because such degrees may not be directly Relevant to the teacher's subject area.

Nevertheless, such degrees also assure the teacher a higher level of pay and are probably not predictive of superior teaching performance.

Following is a copy of an inspirational placard that I maintained and posted on my classroom wall. I sure hope I have been able to consistently follow such wonderfully inspiring quotations.

On Life

"How far you go in life depends on your being tender with the young, compassionate with the aged, sympathetic with the striving and tolerant of the weak and the strong, because someday in life you will have been all three."

George Washington Carver

On Achieving True Success

"To laugh often and much, to win the respect of intelligent people, to appreciate beauty, to find the best in others, to leave the world a little bit better, to know even one life has breathed easier, because you have lived . . . This is to have succeeded."

Ralph Waldo Emerson

On Maintaining a Possitive Attitude

"Every trial endured and weathered in the right spirit makes a soul nobler and stronger than it was before."

William Yeats

"You have to laugh and find humor every day."

Anonymous

Appendix 1

Creative Writings and Drawings

"Lost Someone?"

Have you lost someone who stood right beside you and never denied you? Have you lost someone who always loved you and never put shit above you? Have you lost somebody that always cared and told you she will always be there? Have you lost someone . . . yeh, have you lost someone?

I remember them cold nights and rainy days I lost the one who cared for me. She told me that no one could take my place and her heart is where I will always stay. And I pray today when she's laying in her grave. And now I wish I could see her pretty face. That nigga killed her and shot hisself in the face. Now it's a murder case. I can see the tears running down my Mother's face, so yeh I lost someone on this day.

Have you lost someone who stood right behind you and never denied you? Have you lost someone who always loved you and never put shit above you? Have you lost someone that always cared and told you she will always be there? So have you lost someone? Yeh, have you lost someone?

I was about fourteen years old and my daddy came home and I just knew something was wrong. Then my light came on and I knew he's gone and now he left me singing this sad song. Now I'm doing something wrong.

And this is my very last song.

V. J.

"Love is Like a Bullet"

Love is like a bullet flying through my heart.
The faster that it goes the more it rips me apart.

I cry for you and the pain I feel for you
Could simply make me die.
Won't someone please take away my life
And do the one thing that I can't do.

Oh how I hope this love is true,
'Cause I'm so in love and this love is true.
I am so in love with you.

I won't let you fall, just hold on tight
And make sure all your dreams come true tonight!
I don't know how much of this love I that I can take.
It's not that 1 don't want more,
I just don't want heartbreak.

I don't want to be torn apart and left without a heart
With screaming inside my head
And wishing I was dead.

William

Appendix 2

Gang Affiliations and Identifiers:

The key things to know about Gang Affiliations revolve around three nationally recognized Gangs: The Bloods, the Crips and MS-13.

The Bloods are readily identified through their choice of the color Red.

The Crips are readily identified through their choice of the color Blue.

MS-13 Mara Salvatrucha. Primary color combinations of Blue and Black.

This particularly ruthless gang has its roots in Central America and Southern California.

The use of color identifiers is brought out through gang members' choices of clothing colors or choices of athletic shoes. A 'Blood' will not wear or use anything that is primarily Blue in color (such as a blue file folder). While conversely a 'Crip' will not wear or use any thing that is primarily Red in color. (such as a car).

This seemingly irrational refusal to wear or use items with certain primary colors, such as red or blue, could be a tip-off to a possible gang affiliation.

The other primary method to identify gang affiliations is through gang members' use of graphic symbols, such as pitch forks, devil's horns, devil's tails, the number 6, dice, six-pointed stars, crossed tridents, crowns and/or crescent moons.

Gang members will use these graphic symbols to continually 'tag' things and items such as walls, books and personal possessions etc.

There is an Atlanta-based gang, known as 30 Deep, that has been in the local news a lot doing smash and grabs, car-jackings and assaults, etc. I now recall having seen a lot of 30 Deep tagging within the Paulding detention facility.

Appendix 3

Street Drugs (Slang Names):

Marijuana
Weed
Dooby
Mary Jane
Pot
Blunt
Reefer
Hash
Kush

Cocaine
Ghost
Snow
Crack

Methamphetamine
Meth
Ice
Glass
Quick
Jinkem
Crystal

Steroids
Roids
Hardball
Gas
Hulk

Useful web sites:
www.drugabuser.gov

www.streetdrugs.org

Appendix 4

Designated Felony Acts: O.C.G.A. 15-11-63

Can be committed up to 60 months (minimum of 12 months in a Youth Development Campus)

1. KIDNAPPING
2. ARSON IN THE FIRST DEGREE
3. AGGRAVATED ASSAULT
4. ARSON IN THE SECOND DEGREE
5. AGGRAVATED BATTERY
6. ROBBERY NOT INVOLVING A FIREARM/ROBBERY
7. ATTEMPTED MURDER
8. ATTEMPTED KIDNAPPING
9. HIJACKING A MOTOR VEHICLE
10. CARRYING OR POSSESSION OF A WEAPON (in a public place)
11. STREET GANG ACTIVITY
12. TRAFFICING IN COCAINE (28+grams), ILLEGAL DRUGS, MARIJUANA (50+Jbs). OR METHAMPHETAMINE (28+grams)
13. RACKETEERING (criminal enterprise)
14. ESCAPE FROM LAWFUL CUSTODY (if previously committed as a Designated Felon)
15. SECOND OR SUBSEQUENT ADJUDICATION OF DELIQUENCY FOR HOAX

16. DEVICES (bomb) OR INTERFERENCE WITH OFFICERS. ANY OFFENSE THAT THE SUPERIOR HAS JURISDICTION OVER BUT THAT WAS TRANSFERRED TO JUVENILE COURT: Murder, Voluntary Manslaughter, Rape, Aggravated Sodomy, Aggravated Child Molestation, Aggravated Sexual Battery, Or Armed Robbery with a Firearm.
17. SECOND OR SUBSEQUENT THEFT OF MOTOR VEHICLE
18. SECOND OR SUBSEQUENT OFFENSE OF POSSESSION OF A FIREARM BY SOMEONE UNDER 18 Revised 8/30/07

Appendix 5

Juvenile Court Decisions
(How Harsh?)

Over the past several years there have been numerous articles in the media dealing with the issue and the question posed that for reasons of economy, will **not be printed and quoted** herein. However, I have listed sources information and brief summations regarding the key articles so that the interested reader can easily access each of these referenced articles from the Internet.

"Juvenile Life Terms Before High Court": **by Adam Liptak New York Times, November 8th 2009.**

This article covers crimes committed by juveniles serving life sentences in which no one was killed. Most cases were in Florida. The article notes the extremely harsh penalties that were imposed in order to ostensibly protect Florida's tourism industry. One semi-retired judge even stated that the State's reaction was," out of proportion to the problem and was a hysterical reaction."

"Second Chances" by Raphael B. Johnson Newsweek Magazine October 26th 2009.

The author, Mr. Johnson, relates an incident in which he participated and a man was killed. He had reacted like a typically irrational and angry teen-ager. As a result he spent twelve (12) years of hard-time in prison with much of it in solitary confinement. Mr. Brown relates how he turned his life around by studying hard and reading over 1,000 books! He learned how to manage his anger and ultimately he became certified as a carpenter, plumber, electrician and paralegal! Later on he graduated from the University of Detroit where he earned a Bachelor's degree and a Master's Degree. In the article Mr. Johnson claims that teens should not be judged by the worst things they ever did. He insists that the Juvenile courts should recognize the potential for redemptions is much greater within teens than within adults.

Finally, I wish to direct the reader to look up any single one of numerous relatively recent articles in the news media having to do with the most horrendous and odious scandal of all. Google the **"Kids For Cash" Scandal.** The facts and findings that came out of his case are incredibly disturbing. A prison management and building company in Pennsylvania had paid over $2 Million dollars in "kickbacks" to two (2!) prominent Juvenile Court Judges in Scranton, PA. These "Kickbacks (bribes) were carried out by an attorney for the company who acted as the "Bag man" in delivering cash payment to the judges as a handsome "per head" reward for sending Juveniles to the company were all indicted and then convicted under racketeering and conspiracy laws. What I felt was most disturbing about this was that the so-called juvenile "offenders" were being sent to the worst place they could ever be sent only to ultimately become even more exposed and hardened to a future life of crime. Tragically one juvenile even committed suicide while being incarcerated in one of the defendant's facilities! I strongly urge the reader to search these **"Kids For Cash"** articles on the Internet because they shine a bright light on the ugly temptation of for-profit prison management companies to bribe juvenile court judges at the expense of the juveniles who have inadvertently fallen into the juvenile justice trap. NOTE: One of the convicted judges was particulary notorious for his "**hash and autocratic courtroom demeanor**".

And, finally my response to all those who took the time to register their complaints:

www.ingramcontent.com/pod-product-compliance
Lightning Source LLC
Chambersburg PA
CBHW050412290526

45786CB00003B/1234